ESSENTIAL
TRIUMPH TR
TR2-TR8

ESSENTIAL
TRIUMPH TR
TR2-TR8

THE CARS AND THEIR STORY
1953-81

DAVID HODGES

BAY
VIEW
BOOKS
FROM
 Publishing
Company

This edition first published in 1994 by Bay View Books
Limited, Bideford, Devon, EX39 2PZ England

© Bay View Books Limited, 1994

Published by MBI Publishing Company, 729 Prospect
Avenue, PO Box 1, Osceola, WI 54020-0001 USA

MBI Publishing Company books are also available at
discounts in bulk quantity for industrial or sales-
promotional use. For details write to Special Sales
Manager at Motorbooks International Wholesalers &
Distributors, 729 Prospect Avenue, PO Box 1, Osceola,
WI 54020-0001 USA.

Library of Congress Cataloging-in-Publication Data
Available
ISBN 1-870979-50-8

Edited by Mark Hughes
Designed by Peter Laws
Computer make-up by Chris Fayers

Printed in China

CONTENTS

ORIGINS AND DEVELOPMENT

Triumph had a reputation for sporting cars in the 1930s, and this was revived after the Second World War when the marque, by now a subsidiary of the Standard Motor Co, resumed production with the distinctive Roadsters. Managing Director Sir John Black looked to extend this sporting character, in particular to turn Triumph into a sports car manufacturer comparable with Jaguar, which had used Standard engines in its SS days. His first step was to encourage designer Walter Belgrove with his prototype TRX. This was a blind alley, but it proved fortunate that TRX was still-born because real sports cars were to follow.

The Roadsters, 1800 and 2000, had possessed undeniable charm but limited sales potential. TRX was trumpeted as the 'New Roadster', an up-to-the-minute successor. The use of the Standard Vanguard chassis, basic engine and running gear was sensible, but while the car appeared sleek from carefully chosen angles, it looked odd from others. Construction was complex. It was laden with gimmicks, including electro-hydraulic operation of windows, soft-top, seats and headlights (in this context the notoriety of Lucas electrics in those days has to be recalled). Its cockpit had a bench seat, Vanguard-type instruments and a column gearchange.

Novelty interest meant that TRX was favourably received at shows in the autumn of 1950. Black announced 'thousands of orders' and Belgrove fought hard for it, but other Standard-Triumph executives were less enthusiastic. It never reached production, ostensibly because of the demands of the Korean conflict at the time. TRX would never have been a sports car, but had it come onto the market it could well have deflected Black's interest in sports cars and the TR line might not have been born.

Black was convinced that there was a healthy demand for small, popular sports cars, and believed this was the right market for Triumph to enter. MG was successful with the T-series, and by 1951 (when

The 1800 Roadster evolved from pre-war styling themes, combining mechanical elements from the 1800 saloon with a bulbous body and the oddity of a 'dickey' or 'mother-in-law' seat.

The TRX appeared at late-1950 motor shows (right, in Paris). Publicists emphasised its 'clean sweeping lines' but the bulges and curves were not in harmony – and the unseen double skinning would have made this a costly production model. Boot space was generous, and the lid carried an oversize badge over the filler cap as well as incorporating embryo fins (below).

Black's thoughts took firm shape) Morgan had adopted Standard's Vanguard engine for the Plus Four, and special builder Ken Rawlings had also shown what could be done with a Vanguard engine and other Triumph components in a light and simple car. And the gap in the market between MG and Jaguar was temptation enough.

Black was rebuffed in his attempts to buy Morgan, so he set Chief Chassis Engineer Harry Webster to work on a sports car, which would be styled by Belgrove and would make use of existing components. After the extravagant lines of TRX, Belgrove was constrained by the short wheelbase of the Flying Standard Nine chassis Webster had to use, and the need for simple single-curvature panels.

Henry 'Harry' Webster was an enthusiast whose contribution to the TR series proved fundamental, as Technical Director from the mid-1950s through to the late 1960s. He appreciated sports cars, and in the following years was to find time to oversee Triumph

The sole prototype Triumph Sports Car, 20TS or TR1, at the London Motor Show in 1952 (right), and in the engineering workshops, travel-stained after tests (below).

competitions activities despite his commitment to other Standard-Triumph products.

Something of the basic shape of TR2 was seen in the 20TS (Triumph Sports) that appeared at the 1952 London Motor Show, and subsequently – and conveniently – was dubbed TR1. The decision to exhibit it was taken late, and the little Triumph was overshadowed by the Healey Hundred and the news that it was to be put into production as the Austin-Healey 100. The press reception was lukewarm, and into the following year 'TR1' was rather dismissively referred to as 'the Triumph sports car', while writers enthused about the Austin-Healey. Simply as an exhibit, the weaknesses of 'TR1' – its exposed cockpit, the limited space for luggage, and the nose looking at odds with the tail – were obvious. Others were not so apparent except to those who had access to the stand.

Apart from customary strictures to bear production costs very much in mind, Belgrove had a free hand, and in a reaction to TRX even considered 'traditional British sports car' lines – which apparently would have been acceptable to Sir John Black. But, with hindsight, the rapid decline of MG T-series sales in the TF years shows that the traditional approach would have been disastrous – there was no room in the market for another Morgan. In any case, sleeker body lines were largely dictated by the 70bhp assumed to be available and the maximum speed target of 90mph (150kph), soon increased to 100mph (160kph). So 'TR1' appeared with full-width bodywork, which ahead of the cockpit was to change little in TR2. The cockpit, with cutaway doors, was very open, hood stowage was rudimentary, and there was a stubby tail with the spare wheel largely exposed. The shape was an odd mongrel mix of 1950s practices forward of the 'screen and late-

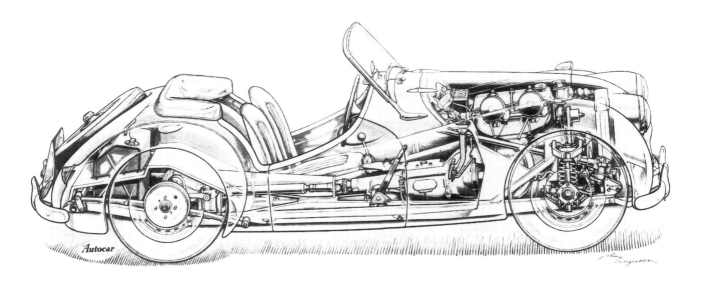

1930s British sports car from 'screen to tail.

Under the skin there was an X-braced chassis (whose origins were in the small Flying Standard saloons), Triumph Mayflower suspension and a Standard Vanguard engine linered down from 2088cc to 1991cc, to bring it within the 2-litre class. Wet-liner construction facilitated this, and also a later enlargement to 2138cc. At least the engine was good, rated at 75bhp in 'TR1' and developed to give a reliable 90bhp by the time TR2 was announced. The chassis weaknesses were soon to become known.

The engine had been designed immediately after the Second World War by a team under Technical Director Ted Grinham and was to be used in the Ferguson tractors built by Standard as well as in cars. The strategy that it should be a multi-use power unit meant that it was simple and durable. Its wet-liner construction was inspired by a Citroën engine.

Meanwhile, the basic price of £555 suggested at the 1952 Motor Show seemed competitive when set against Donald Healey's proposed £850 for the Healey Hundred (although Sir Leonard Lord's estimate for the Austin-Healey 100 was £750), or £530 for an MG TD. Presumably revised costings meant that it was not the figure used in negotiations with possible distributors, most importantly in the USA (early in 1953 Willys-Overland seemed to emerge as a preferred partner, and the possibility that Willys dealers would handle the TR2 was not ruled out until quite late in 1953). When TR2 eventually

The Autocar cutaway drawing was not very revealing as far as the Standard Flying Nine chassis was concerned, but it did show that most of the tail space was occupied by the fuel tank, behind the rear axle line. Luggage was to be stowed behind the seats.

reached the showrooms, that £555 was held, briefly, and the US launch price was $2400.

Realisation of the car's weaknesses came very soon after its debut, and those of the chassis became obvious when Ken Richardson drove the car. He was involved with ERAs in the late 1930s, then with the preposterous BRM V16 when it was still a Grand Prix car (he drove one in practice for the 1951 Italian GP, but the cars were withdrawn after practice). Since Richardson was on friendly terms with some of the Standard-Triumph hierarchy, including Sir John Black and Ted Grinham, and since Belgrove had some early involvement with BRM, the invitation to drive 'TR1' was hardly casual, even though it came on the heels of Richardson's visits to the Motor Show stand.

Richardson's assessment after a brief drive was damning – "it's a death trap" – but accepted by Black and Grinham, who shared a clear view of what was wanted. Richardson was hired in a test and development role, and was later to rally and race Triumph and Standard cars, and run the first Competitions Department. He worked with Harry Webster and John Turnbull, and together they transformed 'The Triumph Sports Car'…

TWO DECADES OF TRs

The TR2 was right for its time. It was simple, it was tough, and there was ample power. Details might be criticised – the ride from bump to bump was perhaps not the best, handling might not have been perfect and possibly there were shortcomings in the brakes – but generally the concept was right, as were performance, equipment level and price. In addition it was to be successful in motor sport in virtually standard form, and early TR performances in really demanding events such as the Liège-Rome-Liège deserve great respect.

By modern standards the total production between August 1953 and November 1955 was modest, just 8628 cars following the prototypes, but TR2 established Triumph as a sports car marque. Sir John Black saw this from a distance, for a palace revolution had ended his autocratic rule. Led by Assistant Managing Director Alick Dick, the board deposed him as 1954 opened.

TR2 resemblances to 20TS were most obvious from this angle. Detail differences included sidelights inset below the main lights, instead of mounted on the wings. This early car, in the unusual factory colour of Geranium, has full-depth doors – the 'long' doors.

TR3 was an improved version, with changes that hardly deserved a new designation, and its rate of sale was little better (13,377). Then with 58,309 TR3As produced, Triumph handsomely overhauled Austin-Healey. However, there was over-production and by the beginning of the 1960s sales were falling, especially in the USA, which was the most important market for cars in this class.

A successor to TR3A was badly needed, but the lead-in was by no means clear. Walter Belgrove's departure late in 1955 was not so critical to the project stage as it could have been, for within months Standard-Triumph executives met Giovanni

A new radiator grille distinguished TR3, and incidentally meant that the guide for the starting handle was hidden.

The restyled nose gave TR3A a lift. The door handles were overdue, and meant that access to open each door was no longer through the sliding rear panel of the sidescreen.

Michelotti at the Geneva Motor Show, and a liaison with the Torinese stylist was soon arranged. Importantly, a fruitful working relationship between Webster and Michelotti developed quite naturally. Indecision about mechanical make-up – engine, chassis and rear suspension – cost time, but business problems became almost overwhelming. Standard-Triumph was debt-laden and the relationship with Massey-Ferguson in the important tractor side of the business was difficult. Dick talked to other companies in the industry, but the turn of the decade was not a time to commit TR3A's successor to production.

Late in 1960 there were talks with British Leyland,

but the subsequent merger proved unhappy. Dick's high-flier attitude offended some of the commercial vehicle men; within months he left, and the merger became a takeover. Dick had contributed greatly to the TR programme, for example in the establishment of a modest Competitions Department and in marketing, but he was probably relieved to quit. Stanley Markland took over briefly, but more significantly master salesman Donald Gresham Stokes was his Sales Director, and was soon to be Chairman of the conglomerate.

Leyland quickly agreed that TR4 should go ahead, and it was announced in September 1961. It had the

The full-width styling of TR4 gave it a more solid appearance than the earlier 'sidescreen' cars. The hard-top looks airy and all-round visibility was good.

same rugged make-up of earlier TRs, but Michelotti's styling was absolutely right for the car and the period. The car was competitively priced and it had the higher equipment level needed to make it more attractive in America. Austin-Healey (with the 3000), MG (MGA 1600) and Morgan (Plus Four) were still the category rivals, but during TR4's life a new breed of hot little saloons was to erode the traditional sports car market.

Triumph sold 40,253 TR4s before the car was uprated with independent rear suspension in 1965. As TR4A it sold another 28,465. Leyland people may have mistrusted sports cars, but credit is due to those who saw potential profits and authorised production (of the Spitfire as well as TR4), and very quickly saw the need for back-up and promotional activities, such as the setting up of a new Competitions Department.

The third-generation TR introduced a new engine in the form of Triumph's 2.5-litre straight-six. This had been developed from a four-cylinder unit for the Standard Vanguard Six, and it had been considered for sports car use in 2-litre form. With the stroke increased to make it a 2.5-litre engine, it was used in fuel injection form in the TR5 and, to meet exhaust emissions regulations, in rather gutless carburettor form in the TR250 for North America. Respective sales figures, 2947 TR5s and 8484 TR250s, underlined the continuing importance of the American market for sports cars.

At this time the Big Healey was coming to the end of its life, the MGB was into its MkII phase, the hapless MGC had been introduced, and there were sundry Morgan variants. The traditional sports car market was shrinking, and Triumph no longer had a price advantage with the TR5, but this model sustained the TR line for 15 months until TR6 arrived in January 1969.

British Leyland had come into existence in the previous year, and there were many calls on its resources. Triumph was an important company in the conglomerate, with a seven-model range of sports cars and saloons, and in the 1970s it was to be given sports car priority over MG. But the development budget for TR6 was minimal, and there were no mechanical improvements of any substance. The German company Karmann was contracted to rework the body, and did so very successfully, the new nose and tail giving it a real lift. The new car looked particularly handsome with the one-piece hard-top that became available in 1973. The larger wheels maintained the 'masculine' image, which had perhaps outlived its time in mass-production terms and was to be abandoned to specialist constructors. Engine ratings went up, but were cut back for the last three years of TR6 when there was more emphasis on smoothness. With hindsight, here was a pointer to TR7...

Cars for the US always had less powerful detoxed

Michelotti's body continued, with embellishments, for TR5 (left) and TR250 (above). Apart from the nose band, the version for North America was badged 'TR250' on the bonnet and behind the rear wheels, where TR5 carried a '2500' badge.

engines, but this market remained all-important. TR6 production, 1968-76, was 91,850 cars, but over a period that was only slightly longer Nissan built more than 570,000 Datsun 240Z, 260Z and 280Z sports coupés, and sold most of them in the USA. Nevertheless, in sales terms TR6 had performed better than any TR beforehand, and it was still listed 'for export only' early in 1975, after the introduction of TR7. And in the opinion of many enthusiasts, TR7 was not a replacement…

TR7 was not the successor Triumph had envisaged before the company mergers of 1968, when British Leyland took over the British Motor Corporation's holding company and formed the British Leyland Motor Corporation. Among its marques were Jaguar, MG and Triumph. In the mid-1960s Triumph had

built a prototype monocoque two-seater code-named Fury, with all-independent suspension and a 2-litre straight-six engine. It looked like a scaled-up Spitfire, and 'in the metal' the scaling-up was not successful. It would have fallen between Spitfire and TR, and in market terms this would have been difficult to justify. Yet a new model in the TR line could easily be justified, and at the end of the 1960s the Bullet project was developed and led to TR7, and thence of course to TR8. Unfortunately, these two-seaters were the only outcome of the programme, for the Lynx 2+2 was to be discarded.

Rationalisation was much more than a buzz word in the confused world of BLMC in the 1970s, but the TR7 programme escaped some of its extremes. However, the sensible intention that it should have

13

Karmann's nose and tail treatment in the quick and economical facelift for TR6 was particularly successful.

much in common with another projected Triumph fell through, as that car was abandoned. In most respects TR7 was a Triumph sports car, but not entirely free of corporate influences, primarily in the body being styled in the one-time Austin-Morris studios. An understandable approach, which turned out to be misguided, was to concentrate on a coupé because it was anticipated that forthcoming US legislation would have the effect of banning convertibles. That did not happen, but it was a long time before a soft-top TR7 appeared...

In TR terms, TR7 was all-new, with monocoque construction, reversion to a beam rear axle and a four-cylinder engine, relatively supple suspension and that wedge-influenced styling that seemed to please few people. As a project it had been well thought through, and alternative engines and transmissions as well as body types were envisaged. Only a few were

introduced into the production programme, most notably the convertible, a five-speed gearbox and above all the V8-engined TR8.

The programme was hamstrung by production problems. The major part of TR production was committed to a large modern plant at Speke, close to the factory Standard-Triumph had acquired and developed at the end of the 1950s. As a BLMC factory the new Speke establishment was completed in 1969, but it never worked to full capacity and became still more uneconomic as BLMC slimmed, while labour troubles further undermined its operation. Months of production were lost, and then more delays occurred when TR manufacture was transferred to Coventry. And all the while Nissan was turning out front-engined sporting cars in numbers other companies could hardly dream of.

The V8-engined car should have been available in

Badging on the TR8 was not ostentatious (the mudflaps on this car are a personal touch), and the last of the TRs had attractive cast wheels.

It has almost become habit to criticise the TR7's lines, but from some angles they were acceptable, especially given the perspective of some dumpy little late-1980s sports cars.

the second half of the 1970s, when the market was still healthy, but it finally arrived in 1980. Although cars with V8 engines had been run by a hard-trying works rally team, when they were known as TR7 V8s, only in North America did the version designated TR8 become available. Ironically, most competition successes came in North American rallies and races, scored by Group 44 and Huffaker cars on the circuits.

With sales of 112,368, TR7 was by no means a failure, and if TR8 had been available earlier it would doubtless have sold many more than 2722. Sales fell away as the 1980s opened: the American market contracted during a fuel crisis and the dollar/pound exchange rate swing in favour of sterling pushed up unit losses, so production could no longer be justified.

The last TR was completed in October 1981. There was no successor to carry the Triumph badge, and very soon the marque was allowed to die.

THE SIDESCREEN TRS

The debut of the TR2 came at the Geneva Salon in March 1952, although production did not get under way until the summer was well advanced. The redesign had been completed by the end of 1952, but testing was limited by time and car availability. Production tooling was in hand through the spring, the first two production cars were completed in July, and through the second half of the year cars dribbled off the Canley line. After TRX and 'TR1' the car looked promising, but motoring journalists still gave it cautious coverage.

Triumph's engineers were inexperienced in sports car terms, but Richardson was there to point them in the right direction. First and foremost, there was a new chassis for which a three-fold increase in torsional rigidity was claimed. The side members were much more substantial, still with cruciform bracing and with more cross members, but with no kick-up at the rear, a feature that was to restrict wheel movement, and cause rear-end grip to be criticised. The chassis narrowed at the rear where the axle passed above it. There were six body mounting points on each side, and some major components such as the front wings were bolted on, which would ease maintenance tasks.

The front suspension was developed a little from its Mayflower saloon origins, and was to become regarded as a weak point. The simple live axle and semi-elliptic springs layout was retained at the rear, with the springs locating the axle. The ride was fairly hard, and while that was still acceptable (even in the USA it was tolerated as part of a 'little foreign car') it would not remain so for long.

The Alford & Alder cam and lever steering had a lock-to-lock reduction, to 2¼ turns; there was a large wheel, and the steering was heavy. The Lockheed 9in × 1¾in drums of 'TR1' gave way to 10in × 2⅖in drums at the front, with improved-ventilation 10in rear brakes coming in 1954, ostensibly as a result of competitions experience, but also in response to user complaints. Plain but not unattractive disc wheels were standard and centre-lock wire wheels optional.

The engine was almost guaranteed not to please traditionalists – those tractor connections were against it – but it was tough and the output was good for a 2-litre unit in the early 1950s. For TR2 it was uprated, developing its 90bhp at slightly higher revs than the saloon version. Larger inlet valves were used, with a higher-lift camshaft, and there were two SU carburettors. The compression ratio was increased

How Standard-Triumph advertised the TR2 in the USA, from *Road & Track* magazine in 1954.

Early TR2s were still referred to as 'The Triumph Sports Car' in manufacturer's releases. The tail lines (right) were not strong, and the slope of the rear deck restricted boot space.

from 7:1 to 8.5:1 and the exhaust manifold was modified. Under-bonnet access was reasonable.

The gearbox also had Vanguard origins with a fourth gear added in a slightly modified casing. Overdrive was to become available, effectively giving seven useful speeds, and this was a major TR plus.

The second major change was in the body, where a longer and squarer tail complemented the nose in overall terms. It housed a good boot, the spare wheel was carried horizontally in a compartment beneath it, and the fuel tank was ahead of it, above the rear axle instead of behind it as on 'TR1'. A little more elbow room was found, but the cockpit was still very open.

When the car had been in production for just over a year, shallower doors were introduced. These cleared most kerbs, and allowed a strengthened sill to show. This change gave rise to the enthusiast distinction nowadays between 'long-door' and 'short-door' TR2s. A fibreglass hard-top introduced at the same time proved popular. When it was fitted, access to the door pull was via a top-hinged flap at the bottom of the sidescreen (the first TRs did not have external door handles). Dzus fasteners secured the flap, and the window above it was in two parts, the rear 'half' sliding to open. Early TRs, as a result, became known as 'sidescreen TRs'.

There were numerous detail modifications through the first 18 months of production, some perhaps reflecting the hasty design work late in 1952. One of the first was the replacement of the aluminium bonnet

17

This early one-owner-from-new TR2 is in original condition, and in this case the plain wheel trims are authentic.

The medallion badge on the early TRs was fairly elaborate.

The TR2 cockpit was functional, and no more spartan than its contemporaries. This car has the early thin-back seats and one of the slender grab handles, positioned so it could be difficult to grasp in a hurry. The clock inset in the lockable glove box lid is not original. Note the generous instrumentation.

Accessibility to the Vanguard-derived 1991cc four-cylinder engine, a notably robust unit, was generally good.

Comparative views of the 'long' (above left) and 'short' (above right) TR2 doors. The stoneguards are in alloy, and tend to be well polished on preserved cars. The earlier car has the simple but attractive standard TR2 wheel, with Triumph's globe badge on the trim.

top and spare wheel cover with steel items, then there were stronger wheels, the addition of steering column braces, and so on.

The cockpit was slightly less roomy than that of the rival Austin-Healey 100 in some respects, but partly because of a longer seat pan the Triumph seats were more supportive. The Triumph also had a more generous array of instruments, and while the T-spoked steering wheel allowed a clear view of speedometer and tachometer, the secondary dials were outside the direct line of sight, and were to remain so right through to TR6. A heater was available in appropriate markets, the fascia cubby hole was lockable, there were small door pockets, and the grab handle provided for the passenger suggested serious intent!

In TR2, Triumph had a real sports car, its first since the superb but ill-starred straight-eight Dolomite of the mid-1930s. While sales far exceeded Sir John

One of the TR2's two cheap boot locks, with its hinged and chromed cover, and the carriage key used to release the lid. A stay supported the open boot lid.

Black's pre-launch estimate, a year into the car's life they were disappointing. In particular, American sales were sluggish, in spite of an enthusiastic reception. Yet the pricing was right. The UK price, including purchase tax, was £871 against £1461 for an AC Ace, £1181 for an Austin-Healey 100, or £794 for a Morgan Plus 4 (the TR-engined Plus 4 was to cost £869). In terms of the then-mighty dollar, TR2 cost $2400, the Morgan Plus 4 was $2600 and the Austin-Healey was $3000.

Contemporary road test reports have to be read in perspective – as a rule of thumb a test of a succeeding model that drew attention to shortcomings was more revealing – but despite differences in fuel qualities the performance figures can be useful yardsticks. In that important US market, *Road & Track* published a favourable early test, but in measured terms *The Autocar* gave a slightly better verdict:

	Max speed	0-60 mph	Standing ¼-mile
The Autocar	105mph (169kph)	11.9sec	18.7sec
Road & Track	103mph (166kph)	12.2sec	18.1sec

These fell a little short of the Austin-Healey 100 (both cars had 90bhp to propel 2100lb), which in *The*

Most TRs looked smart with wire wheels. This TR3 has the later round boot lock covers and similar locks on the spare wheel cover.

Autocar testers' hands reached 111mph (179kph), had a 0-60mph time of 10.7sec and covered the standing ¼-mile in 17.5sec.

Obviously enthusiasts were not overnight converts to Triumph as a sports car marque, despite favourable reports and a growing record of competition successes at levels from club to international. All the while Triumph people, from engineering staff to marketing men, were learning about sports cars, and perhaps that refinement was as important to success as 'traditional' qualities.

TR3 ....

In most respects, TR3 could have been designated TR2A, but that would not have served a useful marketing purpose. It arrived in September 1955, with bigger SU carburettors increasing power output by 5bhp. In 1956 cylinder head modifications (the 'high-port' head) following Le Mans experience raised output by another 5bhp, to 100bhp. The exhaust rasp of TR2 that upset some people was subdued, although

In the tradition of automotive publicity, the designer of the advertisement in *Road & Track* (below) made the car appear just a little larger than lifesize, but this rather haughty young lady gives a true impression of a hard-top TR3A (left).

there was still a satisfying sporty note. Overdrive on the top three gears, introduced on late TR2s, remained optional. Radial tyres became optional in 1956, and when these were fitted retrospectively the improvement in handling was noticeable.

Outwardly, there was a potato chipper grille where TR2 had had a simple opening, and an appropriate badge change. An occasional rear seat arrived as an option on TR3, but it was very small.

The introduction of TR3 was timely, as it virtually coincided with the announcement of the MGA and the BN2 Austin-Healey 100, as well as a fall in export sales. The MGA pre-tax price of £595 undercut the Triumph's by £65, but the TR3 was faster – the MGA's top speed was just shy of 100mph – and the record of competitions in the Triumph's background was beginning to convince enthusiasts who liked to refer to 'pedigree'. During the life of TR3, Standard-Triumph took over the body supplier, Mulliners, which had almost become a subsidiary.

In 1956 Triumph gained a very positive advantage, which was announced at the London Motor Show. At Le Mans in 1955 the works Triumphs ran with disc brakes, and now front discs were introduced on production TRs, a 'first' for a British mass-production model. Apart from a couple of Chryslers and the

Citroën DS19, previous use had been on cars built in minute numbers, and on specialist sports-racers. Girling discs were adopted, and therefore this company's drum brakes took the place of Lockheed drums at the rear. At the same time the Mayflower

The visual lift which the full-width grille and revised bumper gave TR3A was overdue. The wing mirrors are contemporary in style, and the luggage grid on the boot was a Standard-Triumph accessory. The lettering on the nose should correctly be chromed.

rear end gave way to the stronger Vanguard III assembly. *The Autocar* and *The Motor* both tested the same hard-top TR3 in 1957 with the following results:

	Max speed	0–60 mph	Standing ¼-mile
The Autocar	102mph (164kph)	12.5sec	18.7sec
The Motor	109mph (175kph)	11.4sec	18.5sec

Perhaps SKV 656 was properly run in when *The Motor* staff got their hands on it? It certainly weighed a little less. That aside, the extra horsepower had been largely offset by increased weight.

TR3A ....

A year later the next development was announced, as a 1958 model, and although there were no substantial changes this came to be known as the TR3A. A restyled nose was a considerable aesthetic improvement, the wider grille with inset side lights/indicators and less prominent headlights above it giving a real lift. But airflow through it to the engine was not so good, and an internal air deflector had to be added to guard against overheating. At last exterior door handles were standard: the doors could be locked with a key, but they could still be unlocked by reaching through the sidescreen, save on cars with the GT conversion, which had fixed lower panels largely to meet a competitions requirement. The boot lid also acquired a proper locking handle in place of the pair of 'budget' locks. The updating was carried through in details of trim and cockpit furnishing.

Minor changes were made through the following

A left-hand drive TR3A, with, in shadow, the first type of occasional rear seat (the later seat had a straight front edge). The door pulls have been moved inside the trim and are reached in the pocket openings. The sidescreen mounting is hardly sophisticated.

The Italia's lines were up to the minute at the end of the 1950s. Wire wheels were normal on this model, Carello headlights were fitted, and there were separate parking lights and turn indicators. There were no Triumph badges, but the Italia name appeared across the nose and on the flanks at the rear, where it was coupled with Michelotti's 'M' and crossed flags motif.

Built in Belgium by Imperia, the Francorchamps had a different grille style (right), a hard-top and doors with winding windows. In its final form, Triumph's Zest project (below right) had a Ferrari-like nose.

The TR3A spare wheel was still housed in a separate compartment under the boot (above), **and its simple locks remained unaltered from the previous models.**

years, notably late in 1959 to coincide with production changes. Production peaked that year, at 21,298 cars, then it fell as stocks had to be cleared. Triumph was not the first manufacturer to over-estimate the market for sports cars, nor the last…

Variants

In later decades, TR3B in 1962 would probably have been called a 'special edition'. It extended the selling life of the 'sidescreen TR' in North America, where it was sold alongside TR4 and thereby helped reduce stocks. In effect it was an uprated TR3A with a 2138cc engine, which had been used in competition cars since 1959, and in this production form did no more than maintain the 100bhp output, but with a useful torque increase. The all-synchromesh gearbox from the TR4 was fitted. As with TR3A, the

designation was not official and it did not appear on badges. Most of the 3331 built crossed the Atlantic.

Some went to Italy, for Vignale to continue modest production of the Triumph Italia for CESAC, the Italian distributors for Standard-Triumph. The TR3A/B was the basis, and the Italia had a most attractive coupé body styled by Michelotti. Some standard items such as the steering wheel were used in the cockpit, but the instrument layout was typically Italian, with the two main dials ahead of the driver and the others in a line to the right (instead of a central group, which required a driver to look down and across). The windscreen was curved, and all-round visibility was good. The rear seat was even more cramped by the roof.

The Italia sat on 60-spoke Borrani wheels. The boot was conventional, but held no more luggage than TR3's top-loading boot. Tiny fins alongside it held

Michelotti's first TR was perhaps fashionably aggressive in 1957 but overall it was a mess.

This proposal was one TR on which wire wheels definitely looked out of place...

the design together, and the complete car looked a decade ahead of TR3. The Italia was some 220lb lighter than the TR3B, so performance should have been fractionally better. More than 300 were built between 1959-62, with just a handful completed in right-hand drive form. A few were sent to the USA, but this was primarily an Italian-market car.

The only other variant on the first TR body was the Francorchamps by Imperia in Belgium. Imperia built its own last car in 1949, and in the 1950s built Standard Vanguards under licence. The Francorchamps was also a hard-top, with no changes to the basic body lines but with doors modified for winding windows. Only a few were made.

Meanwhile, Standard-Triumph looked to a successor. The simplest project was Beta, really an in-house facelift for the TR3A with a wider track and wings extended to match. Giovanni Michelotti's role

as consultant stylist was soon to prove fruitful, although his first TR ideas car, a 1957 exercise on a TR3 basis, had little to commend it beyond winding windows and some gimmicky details which dated rapidly. But the rebodied TR3 for the Zest project looked forward to the TR4, whereas Triumph's own final Zest had a nose that seemed inspired by contemporary Ferraris, full doors and rather weak little fins at the rear.

Eventually Zest led to Michelotti's TR4, while a project code-named Zoom might have reached production as a parallel top-of-the-range sports car, with a detuned version of the twin-cam 2-litre 20X competitions engine. This was known as the 'Sabrina' engine, named for the shapely bulges at the front ends of its cam covers, after the contemporary TV starlet. The project was cancelled as the company merger with British Leyland loomed.

Sidescreen TRs in competition ....

The first TRs could have been expected to be useful cars for competitions at a club level, for these were simple, tough cars, quick and reliable, available and cheap. Not only did they cost less than an Austin-Healey 100, but as 2-litre class contenders they were less than a third of the price of the much-lauded Frazer Nash Le Mans Replica. The surprise was the international record of the TRs.

But first there were the famous Jabbeke runs in May 1953. These were publicity demonstrations at the behest of Sir John Black, and really outside a motor sport resumé, but they can hardly be ignored. A left-hand drive prototype was painstakingly prepared, although apart from gearing its mechanical specification was largely standard. It was run in 'speed' and 'touring' forms. In 'speed' guise there was a full-length undershield, spats over the rear wheels, an aero screen and a metal tonneau cover, and while the bumpers were removed the standard headlights remained. Ken Richardson oversaw preparation, and drove the pale green (officially blue) car on the Belgian motorway.

The first run in 'speed' trim was made on three cylinders, as a plug lead detached during the approach

John Wallwork shows his driving test expertise as he hurls his TR2 between the straw bales on Morecambe promenade during a winning drive in the 1954 RAC Rally.

to the measured distances, but the mile was covered at 104.86mph. On the second run, with everything working, Richardson exceeded 125mph (200kph). 'Touring' trim meant that the full windscreen was replaced, the metal tonneau cover removed, bumpers

Ken Richardson in the Jabbeke car in 'speed' trim. The bumpers have been removed, an aero screen, metal cockpit cover and rear wheel spats have been fitted, and there's an unseen undertray. The licence holder was removed before the timed runs, but the windscreen mounting brackets remained in place ready for conversion to 'touring' trim.

The first appearance of a TR with 'works' status came in the 1954 Mille Miglia. Maurice Gatsonides and Ken Richardson shared the car (above), which was photographed by Louis Klemantaski, riding shotgun in Parnell's Aston Martin. With aero screens replaced and bonnet straps added, OVC 276 became a rally car, one of the three run by the works to take the team prize in the 1954 Alpine (left).

left off, undershield and wheel spats left in place, and the soft-top erected. The averages of the runs were impressive:

	Flying km	**Flying mile**
'Speed' trim	124.889mph	124.095mph
	(201.005kph)	(199.711kph)
'Touring' trim	114.890mph	114.213mph
(using overdrive)	(184.889kph)	(183.807kph)
'Touring' trim	108.959mph	108.499mph
(no overdrive)	(175.353kph)	(174.611kph)

However much it may have pleased Sir John Black to see the then-recent Sunbeam Alpine figures beaten, the proof of his sports car's all-round qualities really

built up as competitions honours accumulated during Alick Dick's reign. TR2s appeared high on rally results lists from the beginning of 1954, and the car's 'arrival' is quite properly dated in March, with John Wallwork's victory in the RAC Rally, still the 'rally of the tests' in those days, and Wallwork was a driving tests expert. Other private TR2s were second (Cooper) and fifth (Bleakley). Wallwork was later to put in the best performance in the London Rally.

Before the RAC, there was a third place in the minor Red Horse Rally, and good showings in the Hong Kong and Liverpool Rallies. Immediately after, Gatsonides and Slotemaker were sixth in the Alpine (they took a Coupe des Alpes), where all three entries finished and 'Gatso', Richardson and Kat won the team prize. The Lyon-Charbonnières saw Grant and Reece placed sixth, which helped establish the car in international terms, while in British national events there was a haul of ladies' awards.

Triumph gave some assistance to owners, but the cars were little modified. The Alpine team was

Versatility demonstrated. Coupe winners in the 1956 Alpine Rally, with booty on their bonnets (right). Two of the works cars are nearest the camera, the other at the far end of the line. The door handle and chrome strip above it to seal the sidescreen on the nearest car shows that these had the 'grand touring' conversion. The same three cars were also run on the flat airfield circuit at Sebring (below right), but it must have been coincidence that they were lined up in the same order! Richardson is between the cars on the left.

effectively the first works team, although a works TR2 had been run in the Mille Miglia two months earlier. By the end of the year a modest Competitions Department had been set up, under Richardson.

Gatsonides and Richardson had driven that first works car into 27th place in the 1954 Mille Miglia. A works team was run in the TT, alongside a team of independent TR2s – all six cars finished, and the teams were first and second in the teams competition. Edgar Wadsworth ran a private, unmodified TR2 at Le Mans, averaging 72.72mph (117.03kph) in bad weather. This was impressive, but not good enough for it to be classified: in terms of speed it was down

among the French small fry, with a best lap at 84.23mph (135.55kph) and with 104mph (167kph) timed through the kilometre on the long straight. In national racing in Europe the TR did not catch on as quickly as it did among the rally fraternity, perhaps because its tough all-round qualities were less suited to short races on airfield-type circuits than more specialised machinery. However, early TRs became very popular in American amateur racing.

A 1955 highlight was the 5-6-7 finish in the demanding Liège-Rome-Liège (Richardson-Heathcote, Leigens-Rousselle, Gatsonides-Borelly), while the second place in the RAC Rally taken by

The 1955 Le Mans trio, on which disc brakes were evaluated. Apart from aero screens and 'racing' fuel filler caps, the cars were otherwise largely standard. Richardson, in the off-white baggy overalls, is leaning on the 15th-placed car which he shared with Hadley.

Rumsey and Roberts was behind a Standard Ten also prepared by Richardson's Competitions Department and just ahead of another Standard driven by Richardson! At national level there were two victories in Ireland, in the Circuit of Ireland and in the Irish Rally for a driver named Paddy Hopkirk, and there was another crop of regional successes.

Perhaps the Mobilgas Economy Run demonstrated the extraordinary skills of specialists in this odd event as much as the economy of their cars. The 71.02mpg achieved by *The Motor*'s Richard Bensted-Smith in winning the 1955 Mobilgas Trophy in a TR2 – was it his magazine staff car? – was astonishing.

That year the works team ran three TR2s with experimental Dunlop and Girling disc brake systems at Le Mans. They finished 14th, 15th and 19th, Sanderson and Dickson achieving the 14th place at 84.49mph (135.971kph), again well behind a Bristol in the 2-litre class, but not too far behind MG EX182. As a matter of course, the Triumphs were driven both to the circuit and back to Britain.

From 1956, Triumph results were achieved with TR3s and TR2s: for example, that year's 1-2-3 in the Circuit of Ireland was in the order TR2, TR3, TR2. There was another good showing in the Liège-Rome-Liège, with fifth place behind Mercedes, Porsche, Ferrari and Mercedes. There were fifth and seventh places in the Great American Mountain Rally, which

Richardson again (right), this time 'receiving the Standard Motor Company's entrants for the Monte Carlo Rally', to quote the PR department's caption. These TR3As ran in the works team for that 1958 event.

had international status. There was the Alpine, when five TR crews won Coupes des Alpes for finishing without loss of marks (ironically, Richardson's was the only Triumph crew not to win a Coupe). And the level of success in British national rallies was still high – well on into the 1960s a TR was a very economical and competitive car for a private entrant.

Not that works team expenditure was high. Until Richardson's Competitions Department was closed in 1961, economy was necessarily the norm and these early TRs never enjoyed the back-up and development devoted to their Austin-Healey counterparts. Nor, arguably, was it needed, although Richardson's stated objections to 'race tuning' on the grounds that it could lead to unreliability were perhaps too stringent. There was no aerodynamic refinement, and 'competition suspension' just seemed to mean harder suspension.

Consten and Pichon drove a TR3 into third place on the 1957 Liège, on which Triumph took the team award. There was a sixth place and class win in the 1958 Monte Carlo Rally (an event where these Triumphs never seemed able to shine), and a fourth in the Alpine. That year the Alpine organisers abolished

Paddy Hopkirk rashly pushing on towards the summit of the Stelvio Pass in the 1958 Alpine Rally. That rear tyre punctured early on the climb and completing it damaged the engine, leading to Hopkirk's retirement from the event and dismissal from the team.

the 2-litre sports class as such and Triumph ran a larger engine there, and in some other events as well. This change was contrived without difficulty. The original TR engine had been the Standard Vanguard unit and just as its wet-liner construction had been convenient when it was brought within the 2-litre limit, now it was useful in its enlargement. Essentially, Vanguard sleeves (with special pistons) were used to increase the bore from 83mm to 86mm, giving 2138cc. Quoted power remained unchanged, but torque was considerably improved.

Ballisat and Bertaut took that fourth place in the Alpine in a TR3A, behind a trio of hot Alfas, but ahead of the Austin-Healey 100-Six contingent. These places were reversed in the Liège, when Pat Moss and Ann Wisdom were fourth in a Healey ahead of two 2138cc Triumphs.

Successes in lesser events in 1958 included another

This TR3S (right) survived to the 23rd hour at Le Mans in 1959, and was the last of the three entries to retire. The glassfibre bodywork resembled a TR3A in its general lines and many details, although the extended wheelbase was obvious from the side. The 2-litre twin-cam 'Sabrina' engine was a tight fit in the engine bay (above).

Triumph 1-2-3 in the Circuit of Ireland, with Hopkirk winning. By then the works rally effort was running out of steam, partly because the engines were just not developed to keep pace with rivals. There were class wins, and Annie Soisbault's Ladies Rally Championship campaigns in 1958-59, before the summer of 1960 saw the last works sidescreen TRs taking part in rallies…

Meanwhile in racing there had been spasmodic efforts and modest successes. A class win for an erstwhile rally TR3 driven by Kimberley and Rothschild in the 1958 Sebring 12 Hours made for good advertising copy in the USA (never mind that 20th overall was a long way down the field). TRs dominated American amateur racing, numerically and in class results, through the mid-1950s. Then Kastner's successes in West Coast racing in 1959 led the SCCA to change the regulations!

More power came with the 20X 'Sabrina' engine in the TRS, or TR3S, Le Mans cars in 1959. This was a fairly bulky twin-cam straight-four of 1985cc (90mm × 78mm), rated at 150bhp at 6600rpm. A 6in wheelbase stretch was necessary, chassis and back axle were beefier, and disc brakes were fitted all round. The regulation full-width, but low, windscreen made the bonnet look larger, but overall a TRS looked like a TR3, as Alick Dick's policy required it should. Aerodynamic qualities were not good and the TRS was heavy, so the performance gain for the extra 50bhp was modest. At Le Mans all three cars retired,

None of the TRS entries at Le Mans in 1960 was classified, but in 1961 they carried off the team prize for Triumph when the formation finish beloved of publicity departments was achieved: Becquart and Rothschild (25) were 15th overall, Leston and Slotemaker (26) were 11th, and Bolton and Ballisat (27) were 9th.

Construction of the shapely 'Conrero Triumph', planned to have been a 1962 team car, was suspended when the Competitions Department was abruptly closed.

one in the 23rd hour. The first and last went out with radiators broken by fan blades, the other with oil pump failure.

The 1960 cars had minor mechanical changes (no more fans with suspect blades!) and wide-track suspension. The new-shape fibreglass bodies reflected project work with the 'Zoom' and their lines looked ahead to TR4. All three finished at Le Mans, but they were slowed by loss of power resulting from a valve problem and they all failed to complete the minimum qualifying distance. Had they been classified, they would have been 15th, 18th and 19th.

The TRS was little changed in 1961, when all went well and the team enjoyed a staged formation finish. Ballisat and Bolton were ninth overall at

98.90mph, Leston and Slotemaker were 14th and Becquart and Rothschild were 15th. Triumph took the team prize. Construction of a prototype coupé was in progress when the original Competitions Department was abruptly closed. Known as the 'Conrero Triumph', it was to have been the first of the 1962 team cars. Lighter than TRS, it had a Conrero spaceframe, 'Sabrina' engine and TRS mechanical components, with sleek Michelotti body lines. The project was not taken up when a new Competitions Department was set up by Harry Webster and immediately run by Graham Robson. The single car was sold, and the inevitable US-inspired rumours that TRS or the Conrero Triumph would be put into production were simply rumours.

SPORTS CAR FOR THE 1960s

The TR4 was timely, not simply because the TR3 was overdue for replacement, but because the reception and sales quickly justified a new management's commitment to tooling and pre-production costs. Its gestation period had been long drawn-out by the need to make decisions about its make-up rather than any prolonged design phase, for the essential novelties were in body style. Finally, it had to be got into the showrooms quickly to help meet pressing cash-flow calls, so some development details were unfortunately delayed until after its introduction in September 1961.

Various mechanical elements and body styles were considered. Eventually the chassis was carried over little modified and the 2138cc engine was used, driving through a revised all-synchromesh gearbox. At the front the chassis rails were extended to accommodate the 4in increase in front track, but the 3in increase at the rear meant no modifications to the

A TR4 with the optional wire wheels. Giovanni Michelotti's design was nicely integrated, with no backwards glances, although mechanically much was familiar under the skin.

frame were needed, simply extended axle tubes. For the rest, the tried and tested chassis from previous TRs was used. The new body was mounted on it as a single unit, with the gearbox/transmission tunnel welded to the floor and contributing substantially to stiffness. At the narrowest part of the chassis, a pressed steel member linked the transmission tunnel to the back of the instrument panel. Wing panels were bolted on. The bodyshells were built at a Speke factory acquired by Standard-Triumph.

The suspension was unchanged, independent front geometry and even spring rates on the early cars being the same as on late TR3As. Alford & Alder rack and pinion steering was introduced, proving more precise

A TR4A (the version with independent rear suspension) in hard-top form, showing the exemplary all-round visibility achieved with the clever rear window arrangement.

than the old cam and lever type but not much lighter in its first 2½ turns lock-to-lock form (for 1965 the number of turns was increased to 3½, and the steering was lighter). Disc wheels were normal, wire-spoke wheels optional, first a 48-spoke type that was not really strong enough, then a 60-spoke version.

While the 1991cc engine was still listed for use in a 2-litre competitions category, the normal engine was the 2138cc unit, still rated at 100bhp and giving the same claimed, but slightly optimistic, 110mph (177kph) maximum speed as late TR3As. The engine proved to be very flexible.

The gearbox casing had to be revised to accommodate the synchronised first gear. Laycock de

Another TR4 view shows the versatility of the cabin arrangement, here with the roof removed for 'targa' style open-air motoring.

The TR4 chassis was carried over from TR2/3/3A despite shortcomings, notably in the rear axle passing above the main members.

Normanville overdrive was optional on second, third and top gears, and with it a 4.1:1 final drive ratio alternative to the standard 3.7:1 was available.

The new Michelotti body certainly made this a car for the 1960s. First and foremost, it was homogenous and genuinely full-width, whereas in the earlier TRs there seemed to be a glance back to the age of separate wings. TR4 was lower and wider, and its nose was bluffer: in the absence of a drag figure, it is reasonable to assume that there was no aerodynamic improvement. At the nose, a wide grille extended outside the headlights (these had little peaks, in an echo of Michelotti's first TR ideas car), separate parking lights and turn indicators, while the bumper/overriders were similar to those that had appeared on TR3. The bonnet was hinged at the nose, to give good access, and there was a bulge in line with the driver's seat on a right-hand drive car, above the carburettors. An incidental gain was the extra stiffening this provided for that large bonnet top, although it still showed signs of movement…

Full doors were a great advance except for the dwindling band who preferred pre-war wind-on-the-chest motoring, and winding windows made the cockpit snug with the soft-top erected, or with the hard-top or 'Surrey top' in place. The near-flat windscreen of the earlier models gave way to a curved 'screen in a heavy frame.

Michelotti contrived more cockpit room within the same 88in wheelbase. Fore-and-aft, for example,

Independent rear suspension brought major changes in TR4A, in the substantial rear suspension elements and the disappearance of the old X-bracing.

the driver had an extra 3½in of leg room with the seat fully back. The cockpit was fractionally lower, although in exterior dimensions TR4's overall height was 51in compared with TR3's 50.5in. Interior width was increased by 1⅛in despite the thicker doors. TR3-type seats were used until 1962, and the little bench behind them (with optional extra cushion) still provided occasional seating.

The instruments were the same, with the secondary group in the centre rearranged, while at each end of the fascia Triumph introduced controlled fresh-air vents, three years before Ford on the Cortina Mk1. A fresh-air heater was standard. Incidentally, when TR4 was launched it was conceded that the cost of winding windows, including the lift linkage and glass, was no more than the sidescreens of TR3.

The rear deck was flat, making for a boot that was bigger than on previous TRs, but still not large. In a retrograde development, access to the spare wheel was via the boot floor.

The base of the rear seat provided stowage for the 'leathercloth' hood and frame of the soft-top. The

hard-top was distinctive, and overall it anticipated Porsche's 'Targa' top for the 911. The rear window frame was attached to the body, and was sufficiently rigid to act as a roll-over bar. The window gave much better rearward visibility than most conventional hard-tops. The car could, of course, be used in open form. A removable roof panel, in aluminium on some early cars but usually in steel, bolted to the windscreen header rail and the top of the rear window frame to complete the hard-top. The 'Surrey top' option was a soft-top centre section on a light frame.

With a kerb weight of 2184lb, the TR4 tested by *The Motor* was only fractionally lighter than TR3, and with the same power the cars were very similar in performance:

	Max speed	0–60 mph	Standing ¼-mile
The Motor	109mph (175kph)	10.9sec	18.1sec
Road & Track	108mph (174kph)	10.5sec	17.8sec

The TR4 offered just a little more cockpit space than the sidescreen cars, and internal width at seat-back level was unchanged despite the introduction of full doors.

The 2138cc engine in this TR4 has been restored to better-than-new condition. The bay is roomy and the bonnet is hinged at the front.

Comparative nose views show how the parking lights and direction indicators were set into the grille on the TR4 (above left) but moved to fancy housings on the wings on the TR4A (above right).

A black-rimmed three-spoke steering wheel was the original fitting in a TR4 (above). The instruments were clear, but if the bright finish to fascia and glovebox lid did not seem a very good idea, the face level ventilation certainly was. Secondary instruments were better placed.

Tail badge and rear lights of a late TR4 (top), and the TR4A boot lid chrome (above) proclaiming its independent rear suspension.

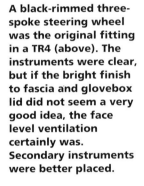

The Motor summed up its report: 'Compact dimensions and an excellent engine and gearbox enable the TR4 to offer more performance than any other production sports car at the price. The body is practical, convenient and roomy; if the chassis design could be brought up to the same standard as the rest, the car would undoubtedly command an even greater share of the sports car market than it does already.'

This was also largely the American opinion from *Road & Track*: 'Our staff never reached unanimity of opinion regarding the TR4. Some thought it was very worthwhile despite its obvious shortcomings – others were not convinced. If past experience with Triumphs can be counted on, the TR4 should be a very reliable car, and it is an enjoyable vehicle to drive. The TR4 offers excellent performance at a moderate initial cost and a sporting driver would search for a long time to

Two ways to keep the rain off one's head (above): the metal roof panel (in steel or aluminium), and the 'Surrey' top with a light frame and soft-top roof section.

Triumph had no works involvement in motor racing with the TR4, but was happy to cash in on privateer successes.

TRIUMPH AT SEBRING '63

TR-4 FINISHES 1 & 2 IN ITS CLASS.
ONLY COMPLETE TEAM TO FINISH.
BEATS EVERYTHING IN ITS PRICE RANGE:
VOLVO, MG B, MORGAN, SUNBEAM ALPINE AND...TWO CORVETTES, TWO COBRAS, A HEALEY, AND A FERRARI!

894.4 MILES IN 12 HOURS.
AVERAGE SPEED 74.5 M.P.H., WITH STOPS.
TOP SPEED OVER 120 M.P.H.
TOP LAP SPEED, 5.2 MILES IN 3:59.4.

IF STATISTICS LEAVE YOU COLD, YOUR NEARBY TRIUMPH DEALER WILL BE GLAD TO WARM YOU UP WITH A FREE TEST DRIVE. YOU'LL AGREE, THE TR-4 IS THE HOTTEST $2849* SPORTS CAR IN THE WORLD.

beat the combination. And, in spite of our criticisms of the car – we don't think the improvements are as great as should have been made – we think Standard-Triumph has a real winner here, if production can keep up with demand.'

Improvements were to come, and as production settled down it did keep up with demand. Virtually all the 1961 production went to overseas markets, and so did most of the 15,931 built in 1962, with roughly one in 15 being released onto the British market. Eventually 40,263 TR4s were built, the last few hundred early in 1965. In 1962-63 its tax-inclusive price of £827 was almost £100 cheaper than its most obvious UK market rival, the Austin-Healey 3000 at £925. Incidentally a Morgan 4/4 could have been bought for just under £730 and an MGB for £870, including tax.

TR4A

Refinement was overdue, and some of it came in TR4A, primarily in the independent rear suspension and improved cockpit, and at a very modest increase in price.

The independent rear suspension followed the Triumph 2000 saloon, save that there was no room for the telescopic dampers used in that car and transverse lever-arm hydraulic dampers were fitted. Semi-trailing arms pivoted on a modified chassis frame, with a single coil spring on the upper face of each arm, to a bridging piece at its top end. This suspension turned out to be almost as soft as previous TR rear suspension had been hard, although by wider standards it could fairly be described as firm. Necessarily, there were detail changes in chassis 'fittings', for example to carry the rack for the steering system (behind the radiator) and extended outriggers for the wider body.

For straightforward production reasons, the modified chassis was also used for the live axle TR4A that was built to meet US distributors' requirements, with brackets added to mount the front ends of the semi-elliptics – the bridging piece was of course redundant.

Tall drivers were not happy with the new seats – these forced a greater knee bend – but the new soft-top was highly rated, for it was simple to erect and secure, and stowed neatly under a cover at rear deck level (rendering that occasional rear seat unusable).

Ride and roadholding were improved, but with its

short wheelbase TR4A could become a little skittish on a slippery surface and rough-road shortcomings were attributed to chassis flexing, scuttle shake still being in evidence.

Detail engine and exhaust modifications increased the quoted power output to 104bhp, but with kerb weight increased again (to 2262lb, with fuel for 50 miles) the measured performance was virtually unchanged:

	Max speed	0–60 mph	Standing ¼-mile
Autocar	109mph (175kph)	11.4sec	18.5sec
Motor	108mph (174kph)	10.9sec	18.4sec
Autosport	108mph (174kph)	10.3sec	17.4sec

The rate of sales did not increase, but it was maintained at a healthy level. In the two and a half years of TR4A production, 28,465 were built, an average of a 1000 a month until production tailed off. Seemingly, about a third of those sold in the USA had the live rear axle.

The Fury could have complemented the TRs had it reached production. It used some TR4 components but was more closely related to the 2000 saloon.

Variants ....

TR5 was to be a straight derivative in body respects, so projects like those of the late TR3 years were not called for. The 'Fury', with a straight-six engine from the Triumph 2000, did incorporate some TR4 components, but was a prototype for a still-born line of smaller sports cars.

Doves of Wimbledon was responsible for the 2+2 Dové GTR4, first seen in 1963. The conversions were undertaken by Thomas Harrington and Co, which had built 2+2 bodies for Sunbeam Alpines. Triumph approved, but its failure to take an active interest was perhaps short-sighted in view of the success of the later MGB GT.

The TR4 boot gave way to a fastback treatment, with a top-hinged tailgate and fibreglass roof. There

was room for a cramped two-person rear seat, which had a folding back so that the niggardly luggage space could be extended. The fuel tank took up the space occupied by the spare wheel in a TR4, the wheel was above it, and the luggage platform above that.

Although it was not quite as sleek as the Alpine conversion, this was a sound project. Between 50 and 100 Dovés were built, and the advertised price was £1250 including taxes, for '0-110mph in luxury'.

TR4 in competition ....

The new Triumph Competitions Department ran a modest rally programme with the TR4. Racing was set aside, in contrast to the US operation, where a race team and an active support programme was developed.

The works coupés were more extensively developed than earlier TRs had been in Richardson's days, and Graham Robson recalls that more than 130bhp was obtained from the engine. Aluminium body panels were used, and in 1963 a limited-slip differential was introduced. But European rallying was changing: apart from a bias against sports cars, the TRs were not suited to many events. For example, the rough Balkan roads used for the Liège-Sofia-Liège meant that the fine Liège successes of the past were not to be repeated.

The fastback Dové was a brave effort, which perhaps deserved to be taken up and refined by Triumph. The rear seats were cramped, mainly by the plunging roof restricting headroom.

There was a fourth place in the 1962 Alpine and a third in the 1963 Tulip Rally, and there were team prizes in the RAC Rally in 1962 and the Tulip in 1963. The last event for an 'official' TR4 team was the 1964 Shell 4000 in Canada, where the cars were run in left-hand drive form and secured another team award. Then the works team turned away from TRs until the second half of the 1970s, when a serious effort was made with the TR7.

The Triumph Competitions Department was resurrected with a TR4 rally team. Here three of the original quartet of hard-top cars are prepared (left) and one is in action in an appropriate setting during the 1962 Alpine Rally (below).

Meanwhile, TRs had been useful cars for amateurs in SCCA racing, although success was confined to just one class championship, back in 1954. With the TR4, support from Standard-Triumph Motor Company Inc was stepped up, a firm basis being Bob Tullius's SCCA Class E production championship in 1962. Tullius's first TR4 was black, and economically built up from two written-off cars.

Tullius was to play an important role in Triumph racing in the USA, with a Jaguar E-type interlude and after TR8 with a wider Jaguar commitment. He started racing with a TR3, moved on to TR4s, and was to win SCCA class championships regularly. With Brian Fuerstenau he set up Group 44 Inc, which ran a highly professional team in a category that was not wholly professional, so it was not always popular. Group 44 was based in Virginia and in its Triumph period concentrated on East Coast racing. Joe Huffaker ran its counterpart in West Coast racing, and went through a parallel Triumph-Jaguar-Triumph progression from TR4 to TR8.

For 1963 there was even an official team for the Sebring 12 Hours, the cars being prepared in America under K.W. 'Kas' Kastner and Joe Valdes. Painstaking preparation, rather than high tuning, helped the team achieve 1-2-4 in its class.

During that race Tullius's TR4 spent some time in

The Group 44 TR4 enjoyed SCCA racing success in the early 1960s. It was normally driven by Bob Tullius, seen here at Bridgehampton with appropriate number.

a sandbank, but he made amends by taking the SCCA Class D title in 1963 (success in 1962 meant he had to move up one category, ironically due to a policy Kastner had instigated, to replace a capacity class system). The efforts of Kastner and Tullius were rewarded with SCCA titles again in 1964–65, and

TR4 service halt at Lochearnhead on the 1962 RAC Rally for Misses Walker and Davis

Charles Gates and John Kelly also won SCCA championships with TR4As. Tullius had a bad season with a TR4A in 1966, the car suffering numerous independent rear suspension failures. Privateer TR4As were 14th and 18th in the Daytona 24 Hours as late as 1967, although quite what the winning Ferrari drivers thought as they lapped the 14th-placed TR 167 times one can only imagine…

'Kas' Kastner initiated a comprehensive support programme for TR entrants in 1961 and officially became competitions manager from 1963, working hard to promote circuit, rally and sprint use of TRs, on into the TR250 and TR6 years. His team's 1-2-3 in class at Sebring in 1965 led to a TR4A being prepared for straight-line use. 'Minor preparation' was permitted for the National runs at Bonneville, which seemed to mean that Kastner could tune his cars to match the output of the European rally car engines. On the salt flats the coupé TR4A recorded 128.2mph (206.3kph), which on reflection was not a great improvement on Richardson's TR2 times in Belgium more than a dozen years earlier, although the TR4A did have full touring equipment, even bumpers. On quarter-mile drag strips, this car recorded elapsed times in the low 15sec area.

THE SIXES

The last major mechanical link with the original TRs was broken when the TR5, with a six-cylinder engine, was introduced in October 1967. The last four-cylinder TR4A had been built two months earlier, but outwardly there was little to distinguish the new model beyond the detail of badges and two coy exhaust tail pipes – even the carburettor bulge on the bonnet remained.

A 2½-litre four-cylinder engine had been considered, and experimental cars had been run with the straight-six in its 2000 saloon form. But one of the objectives was more power, as well as smoothness and refinement, and while it was possible to improve on the 90bhp of the 1998cc 'six' in the 2000 saloon, the 150bhp deemed necessary could be achieved only

This California-registered TR250 is surely too clean to have travelled far along the dusty track. The power bulge carried over from TR4 was superfluous on this model, and those ugly parking lights did protrude...

45

The lines are the same as TR4 and TR4A, but the badges, twin exhausts and wooden fascia mark this out as a six-cylinder TR5, which was built for a limited period and is rare as most production was devoted to the TR250 for America.

Drivers following TR5s could read a catalogue entry (above), but there was just a simple model identification on TR250 (top). Reversing lights became standard fittings on these models.

There was no marque badge on the TR5/TR250 nose, just offset model badges. The TR250 on page 45 shows how this variant's badge was inverted.

The TR250 (left) was effectively the North American market version of TR5, with a detuned engine to meet emissions regulations. Stripes and badges distinguished it. The chrome bar visible at the back of this car is actually part of a luggage grid.

All the spare space in the engine compartment (below), designed for the old Vanguard-derived engine, was needed for the straight-six, seen here in fuel-injected 150bhp TR5 form.

'Rostyle wheels' looked good on TR5 and TR250 (and some TR6s), but they were only trims, complete with dummy wheel nuts.

with a degree of tuning that was unrealistic for an everyday road car. There was also the pressing need to meet the emissions regulations coming into force in the USA, and it was felt that this could be achieved only with a 2½-litre six-cylinder engine, albeit at a considerable cost in power. Hence two new models appeared – TR5 and the TR250 for the North American market.

The engine had evolved through several phases, from a four-cylinder Standard unit to its 1998cc (74.7mm × 76mm) form in the 2000 saloon. Cylinder spacing ruled out a bore enlargement, so the stroke had to be increased despite a general tendency at the time to favour over-square engines. This stroke

increase was considerable, to 95mm, and called for a modified crankshaft, block and bearings.

A new cylinder head was thoroughly tested in Triumph 2000s run with fuel injection in the 1966 British Saloon Car Championship. This was attractive as it offered a possible solution to emissions requirements, while the precise mixture control it provided would overcome problems associated with a camshaft that had extreme timing. The circuit 2000 had very high fuel consumption and characteristics unacceptable in a road car when run with Weber carburettors.

It transpired that the engine would meet Federal requirements with two Stromberg carburettors (sealed

Emissions regulations in North America dictated that the TR250 engine used two horizontal Stromberg carburettors, and produced only 104bhp.

to prevent independent adjustment, except to idling speed!) and this economical solution was adopted for TR250 engines. TR5s destined for other markets had the Lucas MkII fuel injection system, which was reckoned to give a power gain of up to 10bhp, but more importantly made the engine docile in all phases. Incidentally, this was the first mass-produced British car to have fuel injection as original equipment.

Compared with TR4A, the maximum power was increased by some 45bhp in the TR5 – although the 150bhp rating is sometimes considered optimistic – but in TR250 the output was no more than held, at 104bhp. Torque was considerably increased, TR5 having much better acceleration than TR4A, although TR250 figures showed little improvement over the four-cylinder car. In both forms the new car was smoother, and the injection version was only a little thirstier than the old 'four'. American emission requirements were met without hanging additional components on the engine. Incidentally, the six-cylinder engine was 6.5lb lighter than the TR4 engine.

The chassis was changed only in detail, such as having revised engine mounting brackets (the straight-six fitted into the bay neatly), while the suspension was modified to allow for wider 4.5in rim wheels, and the

rear springs were slightly stiffer. The gearbox was retained in its TR4A form but the final drive and the driveshafts were strengthened, as a precaution in view of the increased torque. The standard final drive ratio was changed, to 3.45:1. Disc wheels with detachable 'five-spoke' trims – dummy Rostyles – were normal, and wire wheels remained an option.

The cockpit was improved, certainly as far as the seats were concerned. There were 'eyeball' fresh-air vents and revised instruments in a teak veneer fascia with a matt finish. A padded steering wheel and recessed minor controls reflected US safety considerations, and there was no longer a hard grab handle for the passenger. The folding hood remained excellent and the hard-top with detachable roof panel or 'Surrey top' was still listed.

However, the cockpit was no roomier and the obvious rival in British straight-six sports car terms, the MGC, was bigger in almost every dimension, having, for example, a door-to-door width across the seat tops of 48in compared with TR5's 43½in.

In performance, TR5 at last showed respectable gains, while TR250 offered little improvement over previous TRs. The tests by *Motor* and *Road & Track* were not fully comparable, as the TR5 did not have overdrive whereas the TR250 did:

An American enthusiast was responsible for this 'TR250K'. From the lights flanking the nose intakes it was apparently intended as a road car. If so, it was going nowhere as a production possibility, for the age of impact-absorbing bumpers was not far off when it was built towards the end of the 1960s.

	Max speed	0-60 mph	Standing ¼-mile
Motor (TR5)	117mph (187kph)	8.1sec	16.5sec
Road & Track (TR250)	107mph (172kph)	10.6sec	17.8sec

The *Motor* road test staff enthused about the engine: 'On the basis that high maximum and cruising speed and vivid acceleration are the essential ingredients of a true sports car, this magnificent power unit is the answer to the enthusiast's prayer. Once above its rather lumpy idle it explodes its torque on to the road with effortless ease to the accompaniment of a melodious howl from the exhaust which must delight even the most decibel conscious ear.'

But as that was perhaps a little over the top for a sober and authoritative journal, reservations were admitted: 'Much of the adhesion disappears on wet roads when we found too much power too early sent the back skating away… Full independence keeps all four wheels on the ground under most circumstances and the tendency on bad roads to take off and leap from bump to bump is moderated to a rather untidy lurching on secondary roads. Mechanically sympathetic drivers will be more alarmed by the protesting creaks and groans from a chassis which still

does not feel completely rigid on really rough roads.'

Road & Track summed up on similar lines, with an ominously perceptive aside that *Motor* would probably not have published in the 1960s: 'Offsetting the TR250's new-found powerplant smoothness and interior convenience is a body structure well behind modern standards in terms of strength and resistance to rattles. An entirely new model would have been more exciting to us and to the customers, but the British car industry moves slowly these days and the TR250 is a real improvement over the TR4A.'

As TR5 was launched, the competition was not at full strength. The Austin-Healey 3000 was near the end of its life so TR5 could be regarded almost as a substitute, and the Datsun 240Z was yet to come. The MGC at a basic £895 was a serious rival on paper (but it had its shortcomings, which meant it was not a real threat), and there was the smaller MGB priced well below the TR5's basic £985. The first US list price for a basic TR250 was $3395.

The importance of the American market was underlined by sales during the brief life of this model. Total production was 11,431, falling below the near-1000 a month average achieved with TR4A, and 8484 of those were TR250s, distinguished by colour stripes across the top of the nose. Of the rest, just over a third

were sold in Britain. Customers, it seemed, were not too unhappy, accepting the ride and muscle-testing pedals as part and parcel of a 'masculine sports car', although maybe not accepting 'Joe Lucas troubles' with the fuel injection quite so readily. Because so few TR5s were built, this model has become rare and therefore sought-after even though the next TR might sensibly be preferred.

TR6 ....

Long-term sales prospects in the USA were not promising, and as the TR5 was being launched another move in the leap-frogging TR history – body change, mechanical change, body change – was

Karmann gave the TR6 crisper lines than TR5, although the centre section of the body was not revised. This soft-top on wire wheels looks particularly handsome in Signal Red. In detail, the arrangement of the secondary lights is much neater.

moving towards commitment. This time there was to be a face-lift, and it was to be accomplished quickly, for a TR6 introduction in January 1969. Michelotti's studio was still retained by the group, but its commitments meant that it could not undertake a rush job. Coincidentally, Technical Director Harry Webster, who had played a major role in setting up the liaison with Giovanni Michelotti (and had

A hard-top TR6 on the standard wheels. The stacked rear lights of TR5 have given way to horizontal sets wrapping round to provide the side repeater for the turn indicators.

Front view of the same car shows the earlier type of radiator grille, without chrome trim at top and bottom, used on pre-1973 cars.

important responsibilities for the whole Standard-Triumph range from the late 1950s) moved on to Austin-Morris. So two TR links were broken.

The revamp was entrusted to Karmann of Osnabrück, on the face of it an unlikely candidate but a company with the capacity to undertake major styling and bodywork tasks. There were tight limits on changes, in that the basic body structure had to be kept. Outer panels could be changed, but changes to overall lines were restricted as the existing doors and windscreen had to be retained. It was to Karmann's great credit that the TR appearance was altered just

enough to give it another life…

At the nose the main lights were moved to the outer ends of a revised full-width grille, the wings were changed, and the bonnet-top bulge disappeared. A squarer tail meant a slightly larger boot, and detail treatment was tidier, for example in the rear lights. There were wider (5½in rim) wheels. All this was enough to transform the car's lines, and successfully camouflage the fact that it was unfashionably narrow and fairly long, yet on a short wheelbase. Save in weight, it was not far removed from the first production TR in basic dimensions.

From the land of British Racing Green.

Only 24 of the top racing drivers in the world are eligible to compete in all International Grand Prix.

More than half of them are British.

While for many nations, racing cars has become a national pastime, in England it has grown into a national passion.

For the English, cars are a very no-nonsense, unfrilly business. In a car, they regard beauty as a function of how beautifully it functions, and nothing reflects the English character more in this regard than the classically British TR-6.

It is English to the core. In fact, it's just about all core— a big, beautifully engineered 6-cylinder motor, powering a sturdy transmission that slides solidly from one gear into another.

A heavy-duty independent suspension that can take anything that any road can dish out. All tightly put together in a body with rugged, clean lines and topped off with a couple of comfortable reclining seats to sit in it with

(The only concession to excessive luxury in the car).

The classically British TR-6, is an utterly straightforward, square-jawed kind of car.

The kind they don't make anymore, anywhere but England.

The Classically British Triumph TR-6

FOR THE NAME OF YOUR NEAREST TRIUMPH DEALER, CALL 800-631-1972 TOLL FREE. IN NEW JERSEY, CALL 800-962-2803.
BRITISH LEYLAND MOTORS INC., LEONIA, N. J. 07605

Triumph attempted to woo American buyers with this race-bred slant – but never actually raced TR6s itself.

The 'Surrey top' option was dropped, and the new hard-top was a one-piece item. As before, the soft-top gave excellent rearward visibility, provided the main clear panel was not creased in folding. Of its type, it was easy to erect, but press studs still had to be aligned and this could be frustrating when a quick reaction to changing weather was called for. When it was lowered, the miniscule rear seat was still sacrificed.

New seats were more generously padded, but were not as supportive as their appearance suggested. The cockpit retained its sporting feel, and details were to be revised during the TR6's production life. Instruments were clear, and more modern types would be used when the fascia was revised in 1972. After two years the old ignition/starter key was dropped and the TR at last got a steering column lock. Early TR6 steering wheels had holes in the three spokes, later wheels had a single cut-out shape, and both were more attractive than the padded spokes of TR5 wheels. The pedals still needed heavy pressures, and while the gearchange was positive it was hardly slick, although this was improved in 1971.

The more obvious outward changes that came later were the addition of a spoiler under the front bumper in 1973, while cars for delivery in the USA (in other words most of those produced) had '5mph bumpers'. American requirements, as ever, had led to other detail fittings, such as the very prominent turn indicator repeaters ahead of the front wheelarches.

The revised body was still carried on the chassis frame of box-section side members that was becoming archaic. It was even suggested that Karmann's repanelling contributed a whiff of additional stiffness – but any contribution in that respect was to be

A late US-specification TR6 with cumbersome over-riders (to meet the '5mph' bumper requirements) and turn indicators that appear almost jury-rigged outside them.

welcomed. A front anti-roll bar coupled with fatter tyres improved cornering, giving a more certain feel. There was still squat as power was applied, but little pitch or roll. Overall, the ride qualities fell a little further behind contemporaries, yet they remained quite acceptable to enthusiasts for this type of car.

The same designation was used for cars for the USA and those for the rest of the world, although the PI suffix that had appeared on some TR5 badges was perpetuated to distinguish cars with fuel injection engines. Essentially the straight-six engine was continued from TR5/TR250, with Lucas fuel injection or, for the USA, the less costly emissions-controlling twin Stromberg carburettors. On introduction these engines had the same ratings as before, but the TR6PI engines were to be detuned in the interest of smoothness, so that in 1973 no more than 125bhp at 5000rpm was claimed. However, these were DIN horses; in those terms, the original '150bhp' of 1969 was 142bhp, so the actual 'loss' was 17bhp (DIN). The top speed claimed by the factory dropped proportionally, from 125mph (201kph) in 1969 to 116mph (187kph) in 1973.

As US emissions regulations became increasingly stringent, the output of the carburettor engines was largely maintained. There were carburettor changes, lower compression ratios, a milder camshaft, and measures to consume unburned hydrocarbons in the exhaust manifold. While a 'Federal' engine was rated at 104bhp in 1969, 106bhp at slightly higher revs was claimed from 1972.

The transmission in the first cars was carried over from TR5/TR250, but in mid-1971 the gearbox from the Stag was adopted, in a production simplification which also meant that the TR received a stronger 'box with slightly different internal ratios, although final drive ratios were unchanged. The Laycock de Normanville A-type overdrive that had served so well gave way to the more modern J-type for 1973, and a year later it became standard equipment rather than optional. On the down side, it operated only on the top two ratios.

Early TR6s were tested by *Motor*, *Autocar* and *Road & Track*. The American journal's test of a car without overdrive showed up performance differences between TR6PI and TR6 Carb, while the British tests revealed no great improvement over TR5 in measured performance, perhaps because of the increased kerb weight (the TR6 assessed by *Motor* was some 145lb heavier than the TR5 it tested).

	Max speed	0-60 mph	Standing ¼-mile
Motor	117mph (189kph)	8.5sec	16.7sec
Autocar	119mph (192kph)	8.2sec	16.3sec
Road & Track	109mph (175kph)	10.7sec	17.9sec

TR6 cockpit fittings and furnishings were far removed from the 'traditional' British sports car interiors of early TRs. Clear instruments were set in a teak veneer fascia, following on from the TR5 in style.

Phrases of faint praise were scattered through the *Motor* test: 'The engine is a bit long in the tooth', the car 'can get a bit pitchy on close-coupled undulations but it is well damped and takes single humps and hollows without hitting the bump stops', and the gearchange 'is notchy and obstructive'. Overall the tone for its report was set in an opening paragraph: 'While some other mass production sports cars become gradually tamer and outperformed and outhandled by an ever-faster rash of sporting saloons, the Triumph TR has stood apart from the common herd. In its latest form the TR6 represents what is probably the best value for money in open top terms.'

The *Autocar* summary conveyed mixed feelings: 'Sparkling performance and high top speed. Slow steering, strong understeer, excellent stability. Clutch heavy, gearbox notchy, ride firm. Good weather equipment. Tremendous fun car.'

And *Road & Track* was disappointed to find old wine in the new bottle: 'Triumph surprised us with the TR6. We've been hoping for an all-new sports car from them for some time, but all they've done is update the old one again.' Nevertheless, it was favourable: 'The TR6 does offer a distinctive combination of qualities at a reasonable price: a traditional British sports car package, with ride and

An immaculate TR6 engine bay, showing that accessibility was still good with the six-cylinder engine, here with fuel injection.

The TR6 boot was carpeted and fitted with an interior light. The boot lid has a self-locking prop and the spare wheel is beneath the floor. Notice the impractical position of the fuel filler.

handling far from outstanding and a somewhat cramped cockpit but, offsetting these, an excellent six-cylinder engine, luxurious finish and trimmings, and a top that's easy to put up and down.'

As well as those sporting saloons, and the MGB, Triumph faced a formidable competitor for the TR6 in the Datsun 240Z and later the 260Z. For various reasons, none of the other rivals was as significant as the Japanese coupé, especially in the USA, where they included the Jensen-Healey, the Fiat 124 in its spyder forms, the Fiat Dino, Morgans, various Lotus and TVR models, and even Ford Capris included in the same broad sporty category.

Like the TR6, the Datsuns had straight-six engines, and in US form these were more powerful in bhp/litre terms. The 2565cc 260Z engine was rated at 139bhp, but its torque figure of 137lb ft was little better than the Triumph's 133lb ft. More generally, while the 240Z was no more refined than a TR, the 260Z was improved and civilised, and importantly in some markets it was available with automatic transmission. It was a little larger, and the greater width meant that cockpit space was just a few inches more generous.

The Datsun 240Z/260Z/280Z sold 573,909 between 1969–78, whereas the TR6 sold 94,619 between 1969–76. Despite being humbled in the market by the Japanese newcomer, however, the TR6

achieved tremendous export success for Triumph, since British sales were only 8370.

TR6PI production ended in January 1975, as the TR7 was launched, but TR6 production for America continued for another year and a half, with the last car completed in July 1976, 23 years after the first independent-chassis TRs came off the line. There were no special versions, such as the Italia or Dové, on these chassis.

Development had softened the last TR with a separate chassis, but essentially it was a 'traditional British sports car' to the last, and it sold better than any of its TR predecessors.

Bob Tullius's prominence in US production sports car racing continued through the TR5-TR6 years, with a TR250 (below) and a TR6 (right). The latter car was the TR250 with a TR6 body, and later a chin spoiler and a much more substantial roll-over bar were added. It was demonstrated at Silverstone in 1972, as a lead-in to its London Motor Show appearance.

TR5, TR250 and TR6 in competition ....

The six-cylinder cars were not seen to have competition potential in Europe, at least not until retrospective events a decade or more later, but they were prominent in US national racing. Group 44 ran them among other cars, for example in 1967 entering a TR250 in SCCA events and campaigning Dodges in TransAm. Group 44 continued with the TR250 in 1968, then turned to TR6s from 1969.

The long-stroke, slow-revving engines were a handicap when pitched against the Datsun 240Zs. Group 44 preparation was meticulous, suspension was reworked to a degree (coil spring/damper units were later run at the rear), aerodynamic add-ons were

permitted in 'production' categories, and the TR6s were run with carburettor and fuel-injection engines.

Tullius was injured in a road accident in 1974 and drove the team's Jaguars in 1975, so John McComb took the Triumph drive in those years. At the end of 1975, when he had won the Class D championship, the TR6 was bought by actor Paul Newman, who much later became a partner in Newman-Haas Racing. Newman learned his way into racing with the TR6, started winning in 1976 and gained his first SCCA national title in this car. After this success, the regulation weight penalty imposed on it for 1977 put it out of contention.

This last Group 44 TR6 was later restored to its white colour scheme.

THE LAST TRs

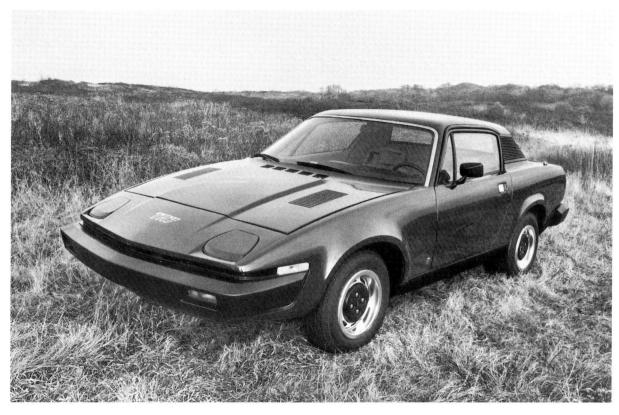

The TR7's designation associated it with earlier TRs, but while that may have had some marketing value, enthusiasts were by no means convinced. Yet in some respects it deserved more than their condemnation, and it did sell more strongly than any previous TR.

Rationally, the departures in concept can be justified. Many of the problems with the car stemmed from the malaise running through British Leyland in the second half of the 1970s, from poor management to unrest on the factory floor at the Speke (Liverpool) plant where the cars were built in a desperately unhappy first phase, with almost a year's production lost. Beyond that, build quality was poor. Production was moved to Canley (Coventry) and then to Solihull in 1980.

British Leyland development funding to create a new sports car for the 1970s was committed to Triumph, at the expense of MG, although at an early

The TR7 owed nothing but its designation to previous TRs, and it has always been the subject of criticism, some motivated by bias, some by its lines. The proportions were unusual, although from this angle the eye is drawn to the ponderous front bumper and side indicator repeaters necessary for the American version, launched in 1975.

stage a badge-engineered MG version was considered. The established TR policy of giving priority to American requirements was followed, a primary corporate objective being to maintain the market share held by the TR6 and MGB, in the face of growing Japanese competition. Research in the USA, which by all accounts consisted of soundings rather than real market research, dictated that the new car should still have its engine in front of the cockpit, and that confirmed Triumph thinking as well as facilitating the use of alternative engines.

The British TR7 that came in May 1976 differed from the North American model only in detail, such as the omission of front indicator repeaters and, of course, its right-hand drive layout. Sue Cuff, Miss Great Britain, demonstrates that this was still a sexist age.

The separate chassis of the TR6 was outmoded, so TR7 was a unitary-construction design from the start. Triumph's one-off mid-1960s project code-named Fury, incidentally, had used a monocoque two-seater design, but this car had been set aside. An intention at the 'Bullet' project stage was that TR7 would use many components from a medium saloon that was abandoned, although parts were also to come from the Dolomite line.

The basis of the TR7 was a platform with strong sills and box-section members to support a front suspension subframe and give strength to the cockpit area and the rear end. A MacPherson strut arrangement was used in the front suspension, while at the rear the simple independent layout of the TR6 gave way to a live axle, from the Dolomite saloon. This was not so retrograde as contemporary pundits insisted, for it allowed adequate wheel travel and damping, while suppleness contributed to generally good ride qualities – which were more likely to please American customers for sporty cars than sports car buffs. There was also noticeable pitch under hard braking – but less movement under acceleration, as that was not vivid – because anti-dive/squat was not a feature of the geometry.

All the front suspension members, and the steering, were mounted to a pressed-steel subframe, to maintain accurate geometry. With the MacPherson struts and coil springs there were transverse lower links and longitudinal location by the ends of the anti-roll bar. The rear axle was located by lower trailing arms, with upper arms angled from the axle giving lateral location. Coil springs and an anti-roll bar completed the rear suspension.

The rack and pinion steering was reasonably precise, and lighter than on TR6. Lockheed 9.75in diameter discs were fitted at the front, 8in drums at the rear. The standard wheels were plain, but then the wire wheels that were optional on earlier TRs would have looked quite out of place.

The drophead TR7 was a long time coming, but generally welcomed when it did arrive in 1979. Its folded hood had a neat detachable cover. This angle shows the rake of the 'screen, and the blind spot problems it could cause for short drivers.

Cutaway drawing of a TR7 in 'Federal' form. It shows the radical departures such as the MacPherson strut front suspension and the rigid rear axle with its location by radius arms. Ahead of the engine radiator fan are the heat exchanger and twin electric fans of the air conditioning system.

TR7 used the four-cylinder Triumph engine in 2-litre form, TR8 the 3.5-litre Rover V8. The TR7 was under-powered, while the V8 in the TR8 was emasculated by American emissions controls, and even had to support air conditioning equipment. The V8 was fine in its normal form in the few cars that found their way into other markets – and of course had the development potential that could have been exploited in the still-born Mk2…

The 'slant-four' Dolomite unit – block and cylinders were angled at 45 degrees – was the basis of the TR7 engine, which had the 1998cc capacity of the Sprint version but the eight-valve head of the standard unit. With two SU carburettors it was to be rated at 105bhp, but the lower compression ratio version with two sealed Strombergs destined for the US delivered no more than 90bhp (and there was only a single Stromberg for California-bound cars). When a

59

The cockpit of the first TR7 was less plush than the TR6's interior. The fascia was a one-piece moulding with a 'leather grain' finish. Comfortable semi-reclining seats were upholstered in corduroy-type brushed nylon. The steering wheel safety pad met US requirements and was not fitted to right-hand drive cars when they came. Instruments behind non-reflecting glass were clear, and this time wired by a printed circuit.

catalytic converter was added in response to tougher emissions regulations in 1977, output dropped to a meagre 86bhp.

The few cars built with the 127bhp 16-valve single overhead camshaft Sprint engine were never listed as a production variant, but the possibilities of that engine were shown in tuning for rally and Formula 3 racing use. Had the TR7 continued beyond 1981, a version of the O-series engine would have replaced the Dolomite unit, as that model had been discontinued at the end of 1980.

The standard gearbox in the early cars was the four-speed Dolomite 'box, notchy and noisy in the TR7, and criticised for its high first and low fourth ratios. Fortunately the engine had a wide and effective rev range. There was no longer an overdrive option, but the five-speed gearbox used in the large Rover saloons was offered as an option from autumn 1976, then set aside during the low Speke period when few cars were built, then reintroduced at the start of 1978 as Canley production got under way, and soon

standardised. The Borg-Warner Type 65 three-speed automatic transmission, the first automatic for the TR, was available on cars bound for the USA from 1975, and generally listed in 1976. But with this, TR7 was a sluggish car, with acceleration in the 'floor the throttle and wait' category.

So two of the main elements were simple and conventional running gear, and a reasonable engine. The in-house styling, by the one-time Austin-Morris studio, was controversial. It might have been difficult to create a lithe shape on those wheelbase/track proportions, and beyond that there was the conviction that open cars would be banned in the USA. In addition, US bumper height regulations coupled with a headlight centre height requirement had to be taken into account, as did the wedge fashion. Ignoring the necessary bumper, the front was acceptable, back to the steeply raked windscreen. The coupé top ended with thick pillars behind the doors and a near-vertical rear window. The boot was reasonably spacious, but it was in an oddly short tail, atop another heavy black

Dark colours flattered the body lines. This is one of the special edition cars, the Premium.

bumper. The whole car looked squat and lumpy…

Dimensions did not altogether confirm visual impressions. TR7 was actually 2⅛in longer than TR6, admittedly with the bumpers more than accounting for the difference. Although on a shorter wheelbase, it was 8in wider.

An open version did not appear until 1979. There were challenges involved in maintaining the impact-resistance qualities, torsional stiffness and light weight of the coupé, and BL was hardly a settled group, but can it really have taken *years* to develop it? It was launched in the US as the Roadster, probably the most honest descriptive name for a TR7. As the Drophead, the open car was introduced in Europe early in 1980, when the coupé gained a folding sun roof. The Roadster/Drophead had to be strengthened, and this was largely achieved with a box-section member welded in behind the seats. Efforts to damp out scuttle shake were not altogether successful – but worse has been encountered in an Italian spyder a dozen years younger. The soft-top was simple to erect, and folded

into a shallow housing behind the seats, concealed by a neat cover.

The two-seat cockpit was good. There was plenty of space and the layout was sensible, the seats were comfortable and supportive, the instruments well presented and clear, and the controls well positioned, but the high scuttle and the steep rake of the windscreen could make for visibility problems. Critics complained that the cockpit was more suited to a saloon, and disliked the black plastic fascia (dark grey in the last two years of production). Early seats had plain coverings, but later there was rather garish plaid material edged with imitation leather.

The coupé came onto the British market at a basic price of £2564, which increased with taxes to just over £3000, some £600 more than an MGB. The basic price of a Drophead in 1980 was £4783, which taxes increased to a shade under £6000, compared with £5164 for the aged MGB roadster.

'Special edition' series came spasmodically, usually with enhanced trim levels or colour schemes. All-

The new interior trim introduced with the drophead was not to every taste, with plaid material in tan or navy.

The fascia was revised for the drophead, looking crisper and more effective in dark grey. The useful stowage trays were retained, and so was the fat little steering wheel with its dished centre.

black suited the car well, and so did the cast alloy wheels that eventually became standard on the open cars. Versions with alternative engines did not reach production (save the TR8, of course), nor did a long-wheelbase derivative called the Lynx, which was intended to supersede the Stag.

Autocar and *Motor* both tested the car in coupé and open forms:

	Max speed	0-60 mph
Autocar (Coupé)	110mph (177kph)	9.1sec
Motor (Coupé)	112.5mph (181kph)	9.6sec
Autocar (Drophead)	114mph (184kph)	10.7sec
Motor (Drophead)	112mph (180.5kph)	9.6sec

In its summing-up of the 1976 coupé test, *Autocar* commented: 'Accommodation and comfort are two of the TR7's strong points; another is the enjoyable way it negotiates twisting roads. It is, for Triumph at least, a new sort of two-seater which may appeal to those who felt that such cars were too stark and uncomfortable for their needs…'

Autocar then felt that the Dolomite Sprint was the real sports car in the Triumph range, but its 1980 test of a Drophead grouped the TR7 firmly with the Mazda RX-7, MGB and TVR 3000M, and, more one suspects on price grounds, with the Caterham Super Seven and the Fiat X1/9: 'It is in all-round behaviour that the TR7 appeals, and though some of its competitors may match it for ultimate handling or offer a little more performance, it certainly achieves a very good blend of sporting handling with comfort, performance and economy, and interior space with external compactness.'

Motor road test staff obviously had mixed feelings in 1976: '…the TR7 is like no TR before. Dolomite engine and simple but well-developed suspension give a reasonable performance and a car that's fun to drive.

Although it was designed to accept a V8, the engine bay appeared fairly full with the Dolomite-derived 'slant-four' unit.

Electrically-operated headlights popped up rapidly, but from any angle except dead head-on they were hardly attractive...

The interior is very attractive and spacious, with lovely instruments, but the car is let down by lack of refinement, an unpleasant gearbox and poor visibility.' Late in 1979, its reaction was much more favourable: 'Triumph's new two-seater is a thoroughly enjoyable, well-developed and refined car with lively performance and reasonable economy.'

Among enthusiasts, comparisons were inevitable, and prejudice built up against the TR7 simply because it was not a sports car in the old manner, which had called for developed muscles and a certain tolerance of discomfort. Yet although it was less powerful than a TR6, on any given cross-country route the TR7 was probably quicker, and only an addict would argue that a TR6 was a more pleasant car to drive on such a journey.

A personal recollection is that a late open TR7 could be a very pleasant roadster. The dreadful build quality of the Speke cars was well in the past, the styling was hardly obvious once in the cockpit (you sat on the 'tartan') and even the visibility limitations became acceptable with familiarity. It was a nice open two-seater – but was it ever a sports car?

TR8 ....

Alternative engines were envisaged at a very early stage, and the Rover V8 transformed the car. The alloy engine weighed little more than the iron-block four-cylinder unit and its use had been planned at an early stage, so no chassis/body modifications were called for, although the battery was moved to the rear. Front/rear weight distribution figures were 56/44 and 57/43 for TR7 and TR8 respectively. The radiator

Only two years before the end of the TR line, the new convertible was still aimed primarily at the USA. Notice the revised nose badge of later TR7s – was this a wreath?

and front brakes were uprated in detail, and there was a higher final drive ratio and power-assisted steering. BL marketing people were convinced that Americans wanted the car with soft suspension, so although the springs and dampers were a little firmer than TR7, for the stiffer suspension that was most desirable an owner had to turn to a specialist tuning company…

For the US market the V8 was supplied in two forms. For most states it had two Stromberg carburettors and was rated at 133bhp. For California it had Lucas/Bosch L-Jetronic fuel injection and a three-way catalyser, and was rated at 137bhp, but with a poorer torque figure than the carburettor engine.

The TR8 was not catalogued for other markets, but the 155bhp output of the contemporary Rover engines is a reference point, and independent

conversions were to suggest that with a mildly-tuned (180–190bhp) SD1 engine a nicely balanced car could be achieved. Much more power could be extracted: in the Group 4 rally car the V8 gave some 280bhp with four twin-choke Webers, and more than 300bhp with Pierburg fuel injection.

In common with the 1979 model year TR7s, there was a bonnet-top bulge, and the cast alloy wheels that were an option on the four-cylinder cars were a standard fitting. That apart, its badges distinguished the TR8, while in the cockpit even the fascia was common to both models. In road trim, depending on specification, the coupé cost $11,000 and the soft-top $10,500, around $1500 more than the equivalent

Crayford's one-off estate conversion of a TR7, embellished in dubious taste with a vinyl roof and Wolfrace alloy wheels.

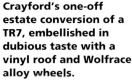

The Lynx coupé, a V8-powered hatchback 2+2 on a lengthened TR7/TR8 platform, might have been a successor to the Triumph Stag, but it was cancelled during 1978.

TR7s, with additional costs for items such as air conditioning (this was a *sports* car?) and emissions tests.

In a road test, *Road & Track* found little to choose between TR8s with the two V8s in performance, save that the fuel-injected car was noticeably more fuel-efficient, as well as California-friendly. The flexibility of the V8 made the five-speed gearbox almost unnecessary. The journal compared acceleration times with the two interesting rivals:

	Max speed	0–60 mph	Standing ¼-mile
TR8	120mph (193kph)	8.4sec	16.3sec
TR7	110mph (177kph)	11.2sec	18.2sec
Mazda RX-7	-	9.2sec	17.0sec
Corvette	-	7.7sec	16.0sec

The TR8 was reported as 'good news': 'Just when it seemed as though we would never again see another mass-produced, lusty-hearted convertible sports car, here comes the Triumph TR8. You aren't going to have to track down a Sunbeam Tiger or older Corvette after all, because now you can buy a brand-new V8 roadster, one that will outrun almost every other sports sedan and sports car this side of $15,000.'

The bright promise was soon to die. Only 2722 TR8s were built, with coupés making up the pilot batch. A convertible came later in 1979 for the 1980 model year, when only convertibles were built.

Sir Michael Edwardes had been British Leyland Chairman since 1977, and in his autobiography *Back from the Brink* (Collins, 1983) he was to recall that the TR7 programme was indeed undermined by industrial action at the Speke plant, and that as the 1980s opened the sports car lines (MG and Triumph) were 'serious drains on profitability'. An oil crisis and recession contributed to the decline in sales in the USA, the essential market. The strength of the pound sterling against the dollar compounded the problem, and of course as sales fell the possibility of achieving economies in production faded, so finally in 1981 BL cut its losses…

There is little externally to distinguish the TR7 V8 or TR8 (below). There is yet another style of nose badge, a '3.5 litre' motif on the flanks ahead of the doors, and a transfer name and designation on the tail (right).

Variants and conversions ....

The TR8 was the only model in a projected range to reach production, and in retrospect it is most unfortunate that the 2+2 Lynx coupé was abandoned. The long wheelbase and overall hatchback lines made for a better-proportioned car than the TR7/TR8, whereas another 2+2 prototype on a slightly extended wheelbase had just looked dumpy. These projects were cancelled anyway in 1978, quite realistically, for however attractive cars on these lines might have been to a small-scale manufacturer (Lynx, with a body in fibreglass, would have been a worthwhile project for a

company such as Reliant), they were not viable for British Leyland as it existed then. In an independent project, Crayford also built a one-off three-door estate car on a coupé base; this did not live up to the reputation built up with the better-known Crayford saloon conversions.

For all the protests about stunted shapes, a bulky rear end, visibility problems for short drivers – the liturgy ran on and on – BL's late-1970s sports car is now desirable. Only a handful of right-hand drive V8-engined cars reached British owners, but a dozen years on several times that number of TR7s had been converted, to quasi-TR8 form. They are not TR8s, or

The V8 fitted in the bay with little room to spare. This is a non-emission twin-carburettor engine in one of only 22 genuine right-hand drive TR8 convertibles built.

The seat coverings in the TR8 cockpit were more restrained than the plaid used earlier in TR7s.

strictly TR7 V8s as that title was used for the works rally cars, but conversions that were conscientious and professional extended beyond simply installing a Rover V8 to elements such as suspension and an appropriately higher final drive ratio, all of which could make the TR7 a more satisfying car.

TR7 and TR8 in competition...................

These cars are often recalled for unlucky rally careers, and BL did put a major effort into a works rally programme which failed to produce victories at international championship level. But that overlooks successes in North America, in both racing and rallying, and if sales really do follow competition successes that must have been more important…

The four-cylinder cars just did not have the power to be major league circuit cars, even in a capacity class. But the TR7 was successfully modified for SCCA production sports car racing, notably by Group 44 and Huffaker, with backing from British Leyland, and was a winner in Class D. Preparation followed a normal strip and rebuild pattern, with components substitution and tuning obviously within the regulations, but to a degree that sometimes seemed to stretch the term 'production'.

Bob Tullius's Group 44 TR7 coupé of 1976 had its engine enlarged to 2047cc and tuned by Brian Fuerstenau to give up to 170bhp, and received uprated suspension with Koni shock absorbers, Minilite wheels and competition brakes. The cockpit was stripped, furnished with a single instrument panel and a single seat, and a roll cage added stiffness. The power output was not quite competitive in the 2.5-litre class (for example when pitted against a Group 44-prepared TR6), but better handling and braking qualities compensated for that shortcoming.

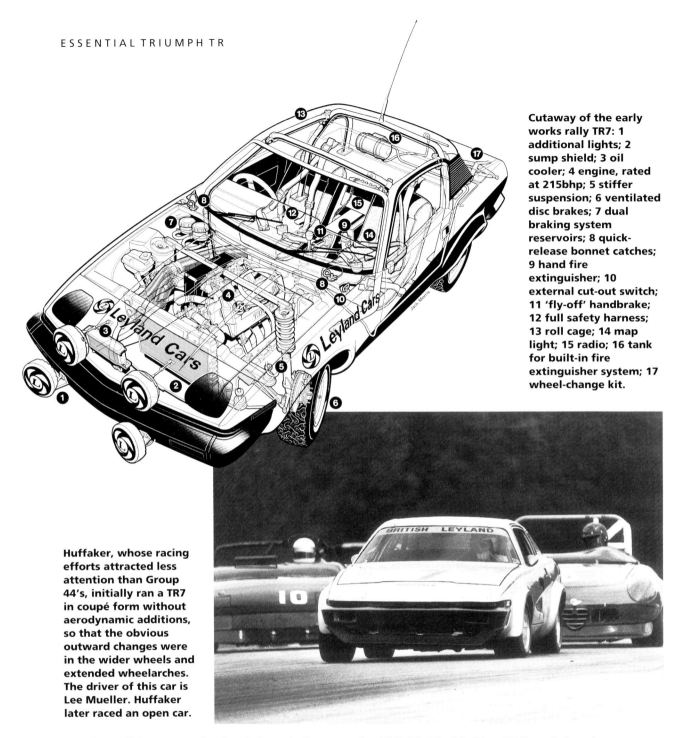

Cutaway of the early works rally TR7: 1 additional lights; 2 sump shield; 3 oil cooler; 4 engine, rated at 215bhp; 5 stiffer suspension; 6 ventilated disc brakes; 7 dual braking system reservoirs; 8 quick-release bonnet catches; 9 hand fire extinguisher; 10 external cut-out switch; 11 'fly-off' handbrake; 12 full safety harness; 13 roll cage; 14 map light; 15 radio; 16 tank for built-in fire extinguisher system; 17 wheel-change kit.

Huffaker, whose racing efforts attracted less attention than Group 44's, initially ran a TR7 in coupé form without aerodynamic additions, so that the obvious outward changes were in the wider wheels and extended wheelarches. The driver of this car is Lee Mueller. Huffaker later raced an open car.

The Huffaker car was developed along similar lines, and, as had become usual, BL's approach was that Group 44 should contest East Coast races and Huffaker the West Coast events. There were also independent TR7 entries in SCCA races in the USA and Canada.

In 1976 the Group 44 car won 10 races from 12 starts, then Tullius moved on to another Jaguar programme in the TransAm series with an XJ-S in

1977-78. The Huffaker TR7 carried on, however, winning in the production sports car series. A Huffaker coupé modified to open form was run up to 1979, and had a Class D Championship to its credit.

Tullius and Group 44 returned to Triumph with a TR8. This was a winner in the TransAm series before the production cars reached the showrooms, and it won again in the IMSA GTO category. Its TransAm performance led the SCCA to impose a substantial

Race and rally TR8s take a break from performance testing by *Road & Track*. The Group 44 racer crouches low and has obvious aerodynamic aids. John Buffum's rally car sits up on purposeful alloy wheels and has no need for added aerodynamic downforce, but the bonnet profile suggests the team had a problem exhausting hot air from the engine compartment.

weight handicap, so Tullius turned to IMSA racing.

This Group 44 car looked very 'special', and it was. Suspension changes and a reduced front track allowed for fat Goodyears, there were ventilated discs all round, a big air dam under the nose, a rear aerofoil, and a NASCAR-standard roll cage. Fuerstenau was responsible for engine development: block and heads remained essentially unchanged, but the bore was slightly increased (to 89.9mm) and a special crankshaft made for a substantial increase in stroke (to 78.7mm) to give 3989cc. A Lucas-based fuel injection system was used, with the inlet manifold from the main-line rally car. This Group 44 engine gave a reliable

330bhp, and 360bhp was claimed for it in high compression ratio 'sprint' form. Transmission was through a four-speed version of the Rover gearbox, and there was a limited-slip differential.

A great deal of work was also put into the rally TR7 and the TR7 V8, which was homologated nearly two years before the TR8 as such was introduced. The BL team was based at Abingdon, where the competitions department had been in the glorious Austin-Healey and Mini Cooper days, and for 1976 it was one arm of a supposedly strong BL re-entry into motor sport, in parallel with the Broadspeed Jaguar circuit effort. Even with the 215bhp claimed for the

Tony Pond, the most
successful driver in the
V8-powered rally cars,
striking a typical tail-
out attitude on the 1976
RAC Rally (right) and
the 1978 Mintex Rally
(below).

The Pond/Gallagher TR7 V8 in the Sutton Park water splash during the 1978 RAC Rally, when they achieved one of the best loose-surface results with fourth place.

The tarmac Manx Rally suited the TR7 V8, and Pond/Gallagher drove this car to victory in 1980.

16-valve engine used, the TR7 simply did not have enough power, and the power band of the engine in this form was uncomfortably narrow. The short wheelbase and narrow track made this a difficult car to set up for loose surfaces, but tarmac performances were promising.

This was proved with the V8-engined car. Engineering Liaison Manager Dave Wood had a small specialist team working on engine development, and the quoted power output of the engine was 285bhp in 1978, rising to 320bhp in 1979. This was a dry-sump unit, with a 10.7:1 compression ratio and initially twin Webers; four Webers and a Pierburg fuel injection system were used experimentally in 1979. Transmission was through a Rover five-speed gearbox, with direct fourth gear, and a Salisbury Power Lok limited-slip differential. Handling was improved with a rearward shift in weight distribution, and by allowing more rear axle movement. Bilstein dampers were used, with Minilite wheels in various sizes and disc brakes all round.

The car was still not good enough on loose surfaces, so Tony Pond's fourth place in the 1978 RAC Rally stands out. Victories came in secondary events, such as the Boucles de Spa in 1977, the 24 Hours of Ypres in 1978 and 1980 and the Manx in

Cockpit of a works rally TR7. The adapted fascia includes a rev counter angled to suit the driver and his electrics 'kill' switch on the centre panel. The co-driver faces his Halda and clocks. The slot in the driver's seat is for the safety harness.

1980. But in the TR7 V8 years, 1978-80, there were just seven rally victories, those in the 24 Hours of Ypres (a predominantly tarmac event in Belgium) being the only ones outside the UK, plus odd successes in the TV-angled Rallysprint, a combination of race and rally prowess. Too often the V8 failed, and the car really was allergic to loose surfaces…

John Buffum was more successful in the less intense world of North American rallying. He ran a TR7 to win the SCCA Pro-Rally series, and that earned him works status for 1978, when he won eight North American events. That success rate continued

The TR7 V8's only international successes outside the UK came with two victories on the 24 Hours of Ypres in Belgium, this being the first, for Pond/Gallagher in 1978.

into 1980, when his TR8 was the most powerful car in the series, with the Huffaker-prepared V8 giving around 280bhp.

The US works-backed activities were then curtailed, and after the 1980 RAC Rally the works programme was wound up. Since then TRs have been active in retrospective events…

TRS TODAY

R ight through to the 1960s, TRs were known as affordable sports cars, and that label holds good again in the 1990s. They were always straightforward cars with a positive appeal, and now there are flourishing clubs and specialist suppliers providing an all-round back-up for modern enthusiasts. The demand for TRs is spread across the range from TR2 to TR6, with increasing European interest and a steady market for restoration work and restored cars, while affection for the TR7 and TR8 is beginning to develop.

TRs were naturally affected by the investment boom that bedevilled the classic car market, to the extent that a good TR6 commanded as much as £30,000 in the late 1980s, while a TR3 with a trace of competition history fetched even more than that. But generally values in the mid-1990s steadied at the 1986-87 level, although now and again a superior auction catalogue might suggest a fancy valuation for a

Well beyond their sell-by date, TRs have been campaigned in historic racing. None has had more success than this brutish TR3A, which the late Reg Woodcock steadily developed during 20 years of competition.

'better-than-mint' example or a top-rate concours car.

As an aside, in the mid-1960s TR3s were offered in the classified advertisement pages of a random issue of *Autosport* for £150-£325. Perhaps they were just not worth advertising in a US magazine with a national circulation at the time, for they seldom appeared. In the 1970s values started to appreciate, and there was an odd reversal of the positions the popular sports cars occupied in the price lists when they were new. Two decades earlier, MG TDs were priced higher than TR2s, and a Morgan was as much as a TD and a TR2 together.

Generally, TRs are readily available, although original TR2s are scarce. Some could be as much as 40

With bodyshell restored and painted, a stoneguard goes back on this TR3, shown in the early stages of final fitting-up at Northern TR Centre.

Rear wing and open spare wheel compartment of a 'sidescreen' TR. All models in the TR family are vulnerable to corrosion, but it takes a prolonged period in the open for wasps to choose to nest...

years old, some fell prey to improvers when they were relatively young and cheap on the used market, while others will have had originality sacrificed with later parts used simply to keep them on the road at a time when little thought was given to preserving them. Much as it might make purists fret, the case for fitting an early car with disc brakes would be strong…

TR3s from late 1956 have the advantage of those disc brakes as original equipment, and that is one good reason for preferring them among the sidescreen cars. Unfortunately, TR3As with all the options from wire wheels to overdrive are highly valued.

There's little to choose between TR4 and TR4A other than the fact that the latter's independent rear suspension would be the enthusiastic driver's

preference. The six-cylinder cars are immensely popular with owners who enthuse, rightly, that few engines sound so gorgeous. Rarity value probably boosts interest in the TR5, but the TR6 has muscular looks on its side. Whereas seemingly nobody energetically seeks early TR7 coupés, the convertibles are now becoming sought-after – and genuine TR8s have always been desirable.

TRs are generally durable cars, particularly on the mechanical side, and in restoration terms they are not complicated. An excellent network of specialist suppliers means that almost every component, even a complete new chassis and bodyshell, is available in remanufactured form, and the few gaps can always be filled with secondhand parts. All the engines are tough and reconditioned units are widely and inexpensively available, while transmission components are long-lasting and obtainable.

Where most TR buyers fall down, however, is in paying insufficient attention to structural condition. Repairs to body and chassis invariably account for at least half of the expenditure involved in restoration, so for happy long-term ownership it is always wise to choose the soundest car available. If the aim is a car that has already been restored, assess the workmanship carefully and treat a photographic record as useful evidence. The body should always sit on the chassis – an ideal jig – while undergoing work, to avoid

Before and after views. Flatting down the primer coat on a TR6 bodyshell (right) after remedial work around the rust-prone seam where the rear deck meets the outer wing (below).

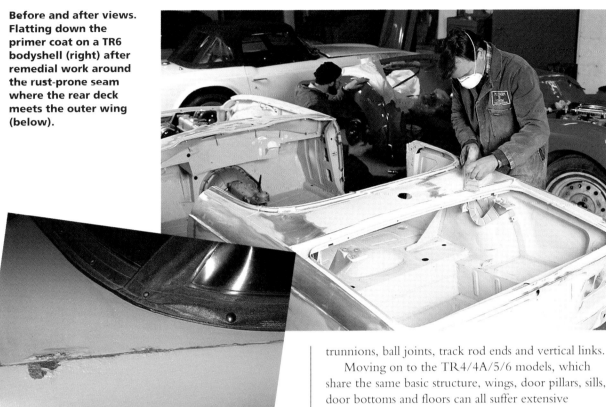

creating a dimensionally inaccurate car with poor panel gaps.

On the sidescreen TRs, any of the outer panels can be affected by corrosion, but this is readily visible. Less obvious points include the body mountings (particularly the two at the front and the four under the cabin), the join between the inner front wings and the bulkhead, the tubular chassis outriggers beneath the floorpan, the junction of A-post and sill, the edges of the boot floor and the inside of the spare wheel compartment.

While the four-cylinder engine is immensely robust, oil pressure below 60lb sq in at 2000rpm when hot indicates advanced internal wear. The gearbox, if anything, lasts even longer than the engine, but bearing noise and an inclination to jump out of first and reverse gears will indicate that a rebuild is due. The only suspension weakness is that the regular greasing required at the front is often neglected, with dire consequences of seizure or severe wear in

trunnions, ball joints, track rod ends and vertical links.

Moving on to the TR4/4A/5/6 models, which share the same basic structure, wings, door pillars, sills, door bottoms and floors can all suffer extensive corrosion. Most of it should be easy to spot, but it is worth looking especially carefully at the whole area around the back of the cabin, where boxed-in sections and complex panel joins can decay out of sight. Bubbles of rust where the rear wings meet the upper deck, for example, can look insignificant, but mean that expensive work is imminent. Bad door alignment can be a useful clue because a car with a weakened structure will tend to sag in the middle.

The six-cylinder engines are almost as rugged as the 'fours', although crankshaft end float is a common problem which develops when the thrust washers wear or even drop out. Oil pressure should be at least 50lb sq in at 2500rpm when hot, and any problems will usually be accompanied by blue exhaust smoke, caused by bore or head wear. On European cars, blackness in the exhaust results from over-rich metering from the fuel injection.

The Lucas injection has been, is, and always will be troublesome. The problems centre around the fuel pump, which overheats and causes fuel vaporisation in warm weather – but there are tales of inventive owners getting moving again by wrapping a pack of frozen peas around the pump! In practice, keeping the

Parts remanufactured for TRs even extend to new TR6 bodyshells, produced in Faringdon by British Motor Heritage. Managing Director David Bishop, who spent many months sourcing original tooling and having new tooling made, shows off the result, along with a finished US-spec car.

tank half-full prevents the problem because the fuel remains reasonably cool. Injectors and metering units do not have a long life, but they can be reconditioned. Carburettor-engined TR6s, of course, escape these problems, but their emissions equipment adds complexity, particularly on later versions.

The TR7's relative lack of desirability, thus far at least, means that the parts supply situation is not quite so healthy. As far as corrosion is concerned, a TR7 has youth on its side, but if body attention is needed there are some items, such as floorpans, where supplies have all but dried up. The Dolomite-derived 'slant-four' engine is cheap on parts, simple to overhaul and fairly durable. Its only trouble area is a tendency to suffer overheating and blown head gaskets, but this usually stems from a lack of anti-freeze causing internal corrosion. Using anti-freeze in the all-alloy V8 is equally vital, but this immensely strong, understressed unit is one of the best engines ever made – and its use by numerous manufacturers will ensure excellent parts supply for decades ahead.

For Europeans faced with corrosion worries, the USA is a good source of complete cars with relatively little rust, provided they have lived in the climate of states like California, Arizona or Texas. Despite the cost of shipment, these cars can be excellent value as restoration projects and conversion to right-hand drive, if required, is straightforward. Few TR7s or TR8s have yet to make the return journey across the Atlantic, but the rarity of good survivors in Europe suggests that more will migrate in the future.

There is a steady if small demand for TR7 conversions. While these do not make a TR8, they can be potent sports cars, possibly over-potent from some points of view. The Rover V8 is readily available and the SD1 transmission includes a better-matched final drive ratio. The engines used in these hybrids, of course, can be free of the emissions-controlling equipment needed on the original cars bound for the US market.

The 'real TRs' have been popular in retrospective or historic competitions and there have been specific TR race series. Some circuit cars have been highly developed, for example with the Lucas mechanical fuel injection system on the straight-sixes replaced with an electronic system.

TR clubs are scattered throughout the world, and can be located through motoring magazines or the TR Register. This is the largest organisation devoted to these cars, with a permanent headquarters building at Didcot, near Oxford. This was formally opened in 1993 by Harry Webster, the Chassis Engineer when the first TRs were laid down and Chief Engineer up to the introduction of the TR6. The Register was formed in 1970 and until the mid-1980s drew a line at the TR6, thus opening the way for the TR Drivers' Club, which still exists although the Register now accepts those unitary-construction models as well. It is very active, organising meetings and competitive events, publishing a magazine and maintaining an archive.

The TR spirit is very much alive.

APPENDIX

Extras and accessories ....

For a series of enthusiast models that ran for such a long time, the lists of TR extras were modest. The most important was perhaps overdrive, offered on top gear at first but from May 1955 on the top three gears. There were a few serious factory competitions components, while at the other extreme a heater remained an extra in some markets through to the TR5. And there were decorative items, such as gear lever knobs in polished wood, which felt much nicer than the standard plastic.

Changes to the body could be made with a hard-top, available for TR3 in steel (which made a good mounting for the Lucas swivelling spotlight that marked out a rally car in those days) or in fibreglass, from the official parts list or from accessory specialists for many years. When a hard-top became an alternative original fitting, kits to convert to soft-top form became available. Meanwhile, Surrey-top kits were also listed, to uprate roadster TR4s, and an optional hard-top remained available through to the TR6. The early TR3 Grand Touring variant, introduced to meet a competition requirement, was a hard-top, and the conversion included 'proper' door handles and locks.

Among other extras that could change the appearance of a car were wire wheels, available 1954-73, and the front spoilers listed by some specialist suppliers in the TR4-TR6 period. Exterior mirrors were catalogued from 1954.

Factory competition parts were available in the TR2-TR4 period, but the list was never extensive. There were no 'performance tuning' parts for engines, while suspension components were limited to competition shock absorbers (TR2 to TR4) and stiffer springs (TR2 only). The latter must have given a harshness of ride that was in period harmony with the aero screens also listed.

Tonneau covers were naturally offered for the open cars, while other cockpit equipment included radios and leather upholstery. Head restraints did not become standard across the range until TR7 was introduced, but they were fitted to earlier cars bound for countries where they were a legal requirement, and they were available in other markets. Seat belts were an extra in home market cars before the TR7. A fitted suitcase and a boot-lid luggage grid were listed for TR2.

Production ....

Some rounded production figures have already been given, largely as yardsticks, but they also make the point that in the overall scheme 'traditional' sports cars were not quite so important to the British motor industry as rose-tinted recollections can suggest.

Published numbers do not always tally. For example, a trifling difference in TR2 totals is presumably accounted for by prototypes sometimes being included. The TR3A/TR3B figures mislead, in that they include the chassis supplied to CESAC to be completed as Italias by Vignale. There seem to be no reliable records of these, so there is no point in including a 'guestimate' in the table that follows. The TR8 total is assumed to include some TR7 V8s.

Model	Years	Production
TR2	1953-55	8636
TR3	1955-57	13377
TR3A	1957-62	58309
TR3B	1962	3334
TR4	1961-65	40253
TR4A	1965-67	28465
TR5	1967-68	2947
TR250	1967-68	8484
TR6	1968-76	91850
TR7	1975-81	112368
TR8	1980-81	2722
Total		**370745**

Technical specifications........................

Details are listed in full for the first model in each TR 'family', with variations given where subsequent versions differ.

20TS ('TR1')
Engine In-line four-cylinder **Construction** Cast-iron block and head **Crankshaft** Three-bearing **Bore × stroke** 83mm × 92mm (3.268in × 3.622in) **Capacity** 1991cc (121.5cu in) **Valves** Pushrod ohv **Compression ratio** 7:1 **Fuel system** Twin SU carburettors **Maximum power** 75bhp at 4300rpm **Maximum torque** 105lb ft at 2300rpm **Transmission** Four-speed manual **Final drive ratio** 3.89:1 **Top gear per 1000rpm** 19mph **Brakes** Lockheed 9in × 1¾in drums **Front suspension** Independent with wishbones, coil springs, telescopic dampers **Rear suspension** Live axle, half-elliptic springs, lever-arm dampers **Steering** Cam and lever **Wheels/tyres** 4in rims/5.50-15 tyres **Length** 141in (3581mm) **Wheelbase** 88in (2235mm) **Width** 55.5in (1410mm) **Front track** 45in (1143mm) **Rear track** 45.5in (1156mm) **Height (hood up)** 51in (1295mm) **Unladen weight** 1708lb (775kg)

TR2
As 20TS except: **Compression ratio** 8.5:1 (7:1 optional) **Maximum power** 90bhp at 4800rpm **Maximum torque** 116.6lb ft at 3000rpm **Transmission** Four-speed manual, overdrive available on top three ratios **Final drive ratio** 3.7:1 **Top gear per 1000rpm** 20mph (24.5mph in overdrive) **Wheels/tyres** 4in (later 4.5in) rims/5.50-15 tyres **Length** 151in (3835mm) **Height (hood up)** 50in (1270mm) **Unladen weight** 1848lb (839kg) **Top speed** 105mph[1] **0-60mph** 11.9sec[1] **Standing ¼-mile** 18.7sec[1] **Typical fuel consumption** 33mpg[1]

TR3
As TR2 except: **Maximum power** 95/100bhp at 5000rpm **Maximum torque** 117.5lb ft at 3000rpm **Brakes** From October 1956, Girling 11in front discs, 10in × 2¼in rear drums **Unladen weight** 1988lb (902kg) **Top speed** 109mph[3] **0-60mph** 11.4sec[2] **Standing ¼-mile** 18.5sec[2] **Typical fuel consumption** 28mpg[2]

TR3A
As TR3 except: **Bore × stroke** 86mm (3.386in) bore on optional engine from 1959 **Capacity** 2138cc (130.4cu in) optional from 1959 **Compression ratio** 9:1 on optional engine from 1959 **Brakes** Rear drums 9in × 1¾in from June 1959 **Unladen weight** 2050lb (931kg)

TR3B
As TR3 except: **Bore × stroke** 86mm × 92mm (3.386in × 3.622in) **Capacity** 2138cc (130.4cu in) **Maximum power** 100bhp at 4600rpm **Maximum torque** 127lb ft at 3300rpm **Transmission** Four-speed manual, all-synchromesh

TR4
Engine In-line four-cylinder **Construction** Cast-iron block and head **Crankshaft** Three-bearing **Bore × stroke** 86mm × 92mm (3.386in × 3.622in) **Capacity** 2138cc (130.4cu in) **Valves** Pushrod ohv **Compression ratio** 9:1 (7:1 optional) **Fuel system** Twin SU carburettors (later twin Strombergs) **Maximum power** 100bhp at 4600rpm **Maximum torque** 127lb ft at 3350rpm **Transmission** Four-speed manual, all-synchromesh, overdrive available on top three ratios **Final drive ratio** 3.7:1 **Top gear per 1000rpm** 20mph (22.2mph in overdrive) **Brakes** Girling 11in front discs, 9in

The original TR2, built between 1953-55, developed 90bhp at 4800rpm, enough for a top speed of 105mph and 0-60mph in 11.9sec.

× 1¾in rear drums **Front suspension** Independent with wishbones, coil springs, telescopic dampers **Rear suspension** Live axle, half-elliptic springs, lever-arm dampers **Steering** Rack and pinion **Wheels/tyres** 4.5in rims/5.90-15 tyres **Length** 154in (3912mm) **Wheelbase** 88in (2235mm) **Width** 57.5in (1461mm) **Front track** 49in (1245mm) **Rear track** 48in (1219mm) **Height (hood up)** 50in (1270mm) **Unladen weight** 2128lb (966kg) **Top speed** 109mph[1] **0-60mph** 10.9sec[1] **Standing ¼-mile** 18.1sec[1] **Typical fuel consumption** 26mpg[1]

TR4A
As TR4 except: **Fuel system** Twin Stromberg carburettors **Maximum power** 104bhp at 4700rpm **Maximum torque** 132lb ft at 3000rpm **Rear suspension** Independent with semi-trailing arms, coil springs, lever-arm dampers (or as TR4 with live axle optional in USA) **Rear track** 48.5in (1232mm) **Unladen weight** 2240lb (1016kg) **Top speed** 109mph[1] **0-60mph** 11.4sec[1] **Standing ¼-mile** 18.5sec[1] **Typical fuel consumption** 30mpg[1]

TR5
Engine In-line six-cylinder **Construction** Cast-iron block and head **Crankshaft** Four-bearing **Bore × stroke** 74.7mm × 95mm (2.94in × 3.74in) **Capacity** 2498cc (152cu in) **Valves** Pushrod ohv **Compression ratio** 9.5:1 **Fuel system** Lucas fuel injection **Maximum power** 150bhp at 5000rpm **Maximum torque** 164lb ft at 3500rpm **Transmission** Four-speed manual, all-synchromesh, overdrive available on top three ratios **Final drive ratio** 3.45:1 **Top gear per 1000rpm** 21.2mph (25.9mph in overdrive) **Brakes** Girling 10.9in front discs, 9in × 1¾in rear drums **Front suspension** Independent with wishbones, coil springs, telescopic dampers **Rear suspension** Independent with semi-trailing arms, coil springs, lever-arm dampers **Steering** Rack and pinion **Wheels/tyres** 5in rims/165-15 radial tyres **Length** 154in (3912mm) **Wheelbase** 88in (2235mm) **Width** 58in (1473mm) **Front track** 49.2in (1250mm) **Rear track** 48.7in (1237mm) **Height (hood up)** 50in (1270mm) **Unladen weight** 2268lb (1030kg) **Top speed** 117.2mph[3] **0-60mph** 8.1sec[3] **Standing ¼-mile** 16.5sec[3] **Typical fuel consumption** 24mpg[1]

TR250

As TR5 except: **Compression ratio** 8.5:1 **Fuel system** Twin Stromberg carburettors **Maximum power** 104bhp at 4500rpm **Maximum torque** 143lb ft at 3000rpm **Final drive ratio** 3.7:1 **Top gear per 1000rpm** 20.75mph (25.3mph in overdrive) **Top speed** 107mph[2] **0-60mph** 10.6sec[2] **Standing ¼-mile** 17.8sec[2]

TR6 (PI)

As TR5 except: **Compression ratio** 9.5:1 **Fuel system** Lucas fuel injection **Maximum power** 142bhp at 5500rpm (from 1973, 125bhp at 5000rpm) **Maximum torque** 164lb ft at 3500rpm (from 1973, 143lb ft at 3500rpm) **Transmission** From 1973, overdrive on top two ratios only **Final drive ratio** 3.45:1 **Top gear per 1000rpm** 21.2mph (25.9mph in overdrive, or 26.6mph from 1973) **Length** 159in (4039mm) **Front track** 50.2in (1275mm) **Rear track** 49.8in (1265mm) **Unladen weight** 2473lb (1123kg) **Top speed** 119mph[1] **0-60mph** 8.2sec[1] **Standing ¼-mile** 16.3sec[1] **Typical fuel consumption** 22mpg[1]

TR6 (CARB)

As TR5 except: **Compression ratio** 8.5:1 (from 1970, 7.75:1; from 1974, 7.5:1) **Fuel system** Twin Stromberg carburettors **Maximum power** 104bhp at 4500rpm (from 1972, 106bhp at 4900rpm) **Maximum torque** 143lb ft at 3000rpm (from 1972, 133lb ft at 3000rpm) **Final drive ratio** 3.7:1 **Top gear per 1000rpm** 20.75mph (25.3mph in overdrive, or 26.1mph from 1973) **Front suspension** Anti-roll bar added **Wheels/tyres** 5.5in rims **Length** From 1973, 162in (4115mm); from 1975, 163.5in (4153mm) **Unladen weight** 2390lb (1085kg); from 1975, 2438lb (1107kg) **Top speed** 109mph[2] **0-60mph** 10.7sec[2] **Standing ¼-mile** 17.9sec[2]

TR7

Engine In-line four-cylinder **Construction** Cast-iron block, aluminium head **Crankshaft** Five-bearing **Bore × stroke** 90.3mm × 78mm (3.55in × 3.07in) **Capacity** 1998cc (122cu in) **Valves** Single ohc **Compression ratio** 9.25:1 (later 9.29:1) **Fuel system** Twin SU carburettors **Maximum power** 105bhp at 5500rpm **Maximum torque** 119lb ft at 3500rpm **Transmission** Four/five-speed manual, all-synchromesh, optional three-speed automatic

Final drive ratio 3.63:1 (four-speed), 3.9:1 (five-speed), 3.27:1 (automatic) **Top gear per 1000rpm** 17.9mph (four-speed), 20.8mph (five-speed), 19.9mph (automatic) **Brakes** Lockheed 9.7in front discs, 8in × 1½in rear drums **Front suspension** Independent with MacPherson struts, coil springs, telescopic dampers **Rear suspension** Live axle with radius arms, anti-roll bar, coil springs, telescopic dampers **Steering** Rack and pinion **Wheels/tyres** 5in rims/175-13 or 185/70-13 radial tyres **Length** 160.1in (4067mm) **Wheelbase** 85in (2159mm) **Width** 66.2in (1681mm) **Front track** 55.5in (1409mm) **Rear track** 55.3in (1405mm) **Height** 49.9in (1267mm) **Unladen weight** 2205lb (1001kg), with five-speed gearbox 2311lb (1049kg) **Top speed** 110mph[1] **0-60mph** 9.1sec[1] **Standing ¼-mile** 17.0sec[1] **Typical fuel consumption** 29mpg[1]

TR7 (USA)

As TR7 except: **Compression ratio** 8.0:1 **Maximum power** 92bhp at 5000rpm; 1977, 86bhp; 1980, 88bhp; 1981, 89bhp **Maximum torque** 115lb ft at 3500rpm; 1977, 103lb ft **Length** 164.5in (4178mm) **Unladen weight** 2241lb (1017kg), with five-speed gearbox 2355lb (1069kg) **0-60mph** 11.3sec[2] **Standing ¼-mile** 18.5sec[2]

TR8

As TR7 except: **Engine** 90-degree V8 **Construction** Aluminium block and head **Crankshaft** Five-bearing **Bore × stroke** 88.9mm × 71.1mm (3.5in × 2.8in) **Capacity** 3528cc (215cu in) **Valves** Pushrod ohv **Compression ratio** 8.1:1 **Fuel system** Twin Stromberg carburettors ('California' spec) or Lucas fuel injection (1981 only) **Maximum power** 133bhp at 5000rpm (137bhp with fuel injection) **Maximum torque** 174lb ft at 3000rpm (168lb ft with fuel injection) **Transmission** Five-speed manual or three-speed automatic **Final drive ratio** 3.08:1 **Top gear per 1000rpm** 26.1mph (21.9mph with automatic) **Brakes** 9in × 1¾in rear drums **Steering** Rack and pinion, power-assisted **Wheels/tyres** 5in rims/185/70 radial tyres **Unladen weight** 2565lb (1164kg) **Top speed** 120mph[2] **0-60mph** 8.4sec[2] **Standing ¼-mile** 16.3sec[2]

[1] Autocar
[2] Road & Track
[3] Motor

The TR4, although very different externally, shared the basic mechanical make-up of the sidescreen cars, its 2138cc engine's 100bhp at 4600rpm endowing a top speed of 109mph and 0-60mph in 10.9sec.

ACKNOWLEDGEMENTS

The writer is indebted to Mark Hughes for his assistance, and the publisher is grateful to all those whose cars were used for colour photography. First and foremost, this book came together remarkably smoothly thanks to immense assistance from Geoff Mansfield at Northern TR Centre (tel 0740 621447) in Sedgefield, Cleveland. This company, whose reputation for restoring, servicing and selling TRs is second to none, provided examples of TR2, TR3A, TR4, TR5 and TR6, as well as the facilities for workshop views. Other cars illustrated in colour were kindly provided by Tom Davenport (TR2), John Walton (TR3), David Tomlin (TR Italia), Derek Pollock (TR4), David Price (TR4), Ken Westwood (TR4A), David Bishop (Dové GTR4 and TR250), Doug Arran (TR6), Margaret and Steve Gales (TR7) and Graham Howes (TR8). Graham Lowe took most of the colour photographs, supplemented by work from Paul Debois. Mike Hazlewood and Bob Haynes, both of the TR Register, guided us towards some of the cars. In the USA, Doug Braden and Beverly Floyd of 6-PACK, the club for six-cylinder TRs, provided a few additional photographs. Sources for historic photographs were David Hodges, Autocar Motoring Archive, Quadrant Picture Library, LAT Photographic, Clive Richardson and Otis Meyer of *Road & Track* magazine.